THE & SWORD
THE MIND

TRANSLATED, WITH AN INTRODUCTION AND NOTES, BY

Hiroaki Sato

The Overlook Press
WOODSTOCK, NEW YORK

to Mishima

First Published in 1986 by
The Overlook Press
Lewis Hollow Road
Woodstock, New York 12498

Library of Congress Cataloging in Publication Data:

Yagyū, Munenori, 1571-1646.
The sword and the mind.

Translation of: Hyōhō kadensho.
Includes index.
1. Swordplay—Japan—Philosophy—Early works to 1800.
2. Military art and science—Japan—Early works to 1800.
I. Tittle.
U101 .Y3413   1895   796.8'6'0952   85-8899

ISBN 0-87951-209-1 (hardcover)
ISBN 0-87951-256-3 (paperback)

Seventh Printing, 2000

Contents

BOOKS BY HIROAKI SATO

One Hundred Frogs: From Renga to Haiku to English

Translations:

Poems of Princess Shikishi
Ten Japanese Poets
Spring & Asura: Poems of Kenji Miyazawa
Mutsuo Takahashi: Poems of a Penisist
Lilac Garden: Poems of Minoru Yoshioka
Howling at the Moon: Poems of Hagiwara Sakutarō
See You Soon: Poems of Taeko Tomioka
Chieko and Other Poems of Takamura Kōtarō
A Bunch of Keys: Poems of Mutsuo Takahashi

with Burton Watson
From the Country of Eight Islands: An Anthology of Japanese Poetry

Note and Acknowledgments

In translating the *Heibō Kaden Sho*, the centerpiece of this book, I was greatly aided by Watanabe Ichirō's text in *Kinsei Geidō Ron*, a selection of treatises on the arts published by Iwanami Shoten in 1972; among the several texts in print, it is, to my knowledge, the only one annotated. I hope the notes I have added on my own are equally relevant and free of errors. I also learned much about Japanese swordsmanship and the Yagyū contribution to it from another eminent scholar, Imamura Yoshio. A professor of athletics, Imamura has done a great deal to take swordsmanship out of the domain of popular fantasy.

I am indebted to several other persons. Yagyū Munenori, the fifteenth generation of the Yagyū family, encouraged me all along and provided valuable books. Kinoshita Tetsuo spent many hours for me trying to obtain permission for the use of illustrative material; it was through him that the Tōkai temple graciously allowed the use of the Zen monk Takuan's famous calligraphy. Yamamoto Kōzō photographed the Hōtoku temple and other places related to the Yagyū. Mishima Hiroaki assembled several books on Takuan and his writings. Kakizaki Seiji (or Seiji Kakizaki, as he is known as a New York photographer) prepared excellent photographic reproductions of the *Shinkage-ryū Heibō Mokuroku,* by permission of Iwanami Shoten. Burton Watson spelled the Chinese names for me. Hirata Takako and Yano Sumiko routinely helped obtain needed books and information; had they not been as willing and prompt as they were, this book would not have come into being. Robert Fagan, as always, helped me revise the manuscript. I am nonetheless to blame for all the awkward spots that may remain—not to mention all the possible interpretive errors.

I have tried to maintain fidelity to the original in translating the texts in this book, as I have elsewhere. Most of the section headings are mine, however, and the bracketed explanations are either my additions or excerpts from the writings of Yagyū men other than Munenori. The sources of the excerpts are not indicated, other than the names of those who wrote the quoted words, because the ordinary reader is unlikely to go to the sources, although it should be easy to locate them should the reader decide to do so. It was not possible to translate certain key words and phrases consistently throughout. The best example is the word *heibō* (also pronounced *hyōbō*): it may mean swordsmanship, sword fight, stratagem, strategy, tactics, the art of war. When any of these words appears in the translation of the *Heibō Kaden Sho,* the reader may assume that the original word is *heibō.*

The footnotes are numbered consecutively throughout the Introduction; page by page elsewhere.

All the Japanese names are given in Japanese fashion, the family name first. the only exception is my own, which is given in the Occidental manner.

Dream

> *One hundred years, thirty-six*
> *thousand days. Maitreya, Avalokitésvara,*
> *how many yeses and nos? Yes is also a dream.*
> *No is also a dream. Maitreya is a dream. Avoloki-*
> *tésvara is also a dream. The Buddha said, "So is all*
> *to be seen."*
> *Takuan the old rustic abruptly took up the brush.*

The official life of Takuan, known as *Tōkai Oshō Kinen Roku,* has this entry for the twelfth month, 1645: "11th day, hour of the tiger. The people of the temple requested his death verse. The teacher waved his hand and would not listen. They practically forced him. He then took up the brush, wrote the single character Dream, threw away the brush, and passed on." The entry makes no mention of the verse.

In the verse, the first half of the third line is said to be ambiguous; the sentence, if it is one, may mean, "How often have even the revered and enlightened Maitreya and Avalokitesvara said yes and no?" The quotation at the end refers to a famous statement in *The Diamond Sutra:* "Every phenomenon is like a dream, an illusion, a bubble, a shadow; it is like dew and also like lightning. So is all to be seen."

Chronology of Japanese History

to ca. A.D. 700:   **Early Period**

    ca. 350 A.D.:   Formation of the Japanese state(?)

    early sixth century: Introduction of Buddhism from Korea

    607:   First embassy to China

    702:   First law codes promulgated

700 to 1200:   **The Aristocratic Period**

    710:   Capital established at Nara

    794:   Capital moved to Kyoto

    early eleventh century: *The Tale of Genji* written by Lady Murasaki

    1180-1185:   War between the two military clans, Minamoto and Taira

1200 to 1868:   **The Feudal Period**

    1192:   Minamoto no Yoritomo sets up his administration in Kamakura and is granted the title of *shogun*

    1467-1477:   Ōnin war. [The period of about a hundred years beginning with the Ōnin war is known as **The Age of Warring States**]

    1603:   Tokugawa Ieyasu sets up his administration in Edo (present-day Tokyo) and is granted the title of *shogun*

    1853:   Commodore Perry arrives in Japan

1868 to Present: **The Modern Period**

    1868:   Rule by the emperor resumed

    1941-1945:   Pacific War; surrender of Japan

    1946:   Parliamentary government established

Chronology of Yagyū-Related Events

[From *The Age of Warring States*
to the Establishment of the *Tokugawa Shogunate*]

1467 to 1477:   Ōnin War (civil war)

ca. 1508:   Swordsman **Kamiizumi Hidetsuna** born.

1529:   Swordsman **Yagyū Muneyoshi** born.

1542 or 1543:   The harquebus (matchlock) accidentally reaches Japan from Portugal.

1563:   **Hidetsuna**, defeated in a territorial war, becomes an independent swordsman.

1565:   **Hidetsuna** teaches the Shinkage school of swordsmanship to **Muneyoshi**.

1568:   Warlord **Oda Nobunaga** occupies the imperial capital of Kyoto.

1571:   Swordsman **Yagyū Munenori** born.

1575:   **Nobunaga** defeats **Takeda Katsuyori** through a strategic deployment of the harquebus.

1577:   **Hidetsuna** dies.

1582:   **Nobunaga** assassinated; **Toyotomi Hideyoshi**, one of his generals, takes over.

1590:   **Hideyoshi** gains control of the country.

1594:   **Muneyoshi** and **Munenori** meet **Tokugawa Ieyasu**, then **Hideyoshi**'s top aide; **Ieyasu** becomes **Muneyoshi**'s student.

1598:   **Hideyoshi** dies.

1600:   Battle of Sekigahara, wherein practically all the warlords split into two groups and clash; **Ieyasu**, leader of the Eastern Group, emerges victorious.

1603:   Title of *shogun* granted to **Ieyasu**.

1606:   **Muneyoshi** dies.

1607:   **Munenori**'s first son, **Mitsuyoshi**, born.

1614-1615:   Osaka summer and winter campaigns; **Toyotomi** family destroyed.

1616:   **Ieyasu** dies.

1623:   **Iemitsu** becomes third Tokugawa shogun and solidifies the institutional foundations of Tokugawa government; **Munenori** becomes his instructor of swordsmanship.

1629:   Zen monk **Takuan** exiled.

1632: **Takuan** pardoned upon second shogun **Hidetada**'s death; **Munenori** completes his treatise on swordsmanship, *Heihō Kaden Sho;* the position of ō-*metsuke* created, with **Munenori** among the first officials to be appointed to it.

1636: **Munenori**'s holdings reach 10,000 *koku,* making him a daimyo.

1637: Religious uprisings in Shimabara, Kyushu; quelled the next year.

1639: Seclusion policy completed. [From then on, until Commodore Perry's arrival in 1853, only small numbers of Dutch, Chinese, and Koreans are admitted into Japan.]

1645: Swordsman **Miyamoto Musashi** completes his treatise on swordsmanship, *Gorin no Sho* (A Book of Five Rings) and dies shortly afterward; **Takuan** dies.

1646: **Munenori** dies.

1651: **Iemitsu** dies.

Introduction

The *Heibō Kaden Sho* (Family-Transmitted Book on Swordsmanship), a complete translation of which makes up the main body of this book, contains the observations of three swordsmen: Kamiizumi Hidetsuna (1508?-1588), Yagyū Muneyoshi (1529-1606), and Muneyoshi's son, Munenori (1571-1646). During the century and a half that these three men lived, Japan changed fundamentally. When Hidetsuna was born, the country was in the middle of the age of warring states. By the time Munenori died, the foundations of the Tokugawa shogunate (1603-1868) had been firmly laid, and the domestic stability of the country has never been seriously broken since. The three men's lives illustrate the historic changes that took place throughout these years.

Three Swordsmen

HIDETSUNA. The Kamiizumi, of which Hidetsuna was a member, was a local clan that served the Uesugi family. The Uesugi, in turn, served the Ashikaga shogunate (1338–1572), first as administrative assistants to the shogun and later as governors of the Kanto region—present-day Tokyo and its surrounding areas. But the power and prestige of the Ashikaga had been badly reduced in the Ōnin War (1467–1477), and was never to recover. The same fate befell the Uesugi, even though as governor of Kanto the head of the family had the status of overlord. In 1552, when a local warlord attacked and drove Uesugi Norimasa out of the region, Hidetsuna surrendered his fort and pledged allegiance to the victor.

Hidetsuna, however, secretly kept in touch with Nagao Kagetora (1530–1578), the lord of a nearby region to whom Narimasa had turned for help.[1] When Kagetora's forces regained part of Norimasa's territory, Hidetsuna was placed under the command of one of Kagetora's generals. It was while working for that general that he distinguished himself as a warrior. In one battle he speared the enemy commander and was given the title of "best spearman." In 1563 the same area was taken by Kagetora's arch rival, Takeda Shingen (1521–1573). According to an account of the Takeda clan's military exploits, Hidetsuna joined Shingen's army, along with two hundred other defeated warriors.

Soon afterward Hidetsuna asked to be relieved of his duties. Despite Shingen's pleadings, he left the region to travel the country in order to perfect his swordsmanship. Two episodes told of him after he decided to become a professional swordsman are noteworthy.

One of them has to do with riceballs. As Hidetsuna and his retinue of five men, which included his son and a student swordsman, Hikita Toyogorō, approached the Myōkō temple in Owari, they came across a crowd of villagers who were anxious and confused about something. Upon inquiry, it was learned that a desperado had taken a child hostage, installed himself along with his hostage in a barn, and was threatening to kill the child with his sword if anyone came near him. The child's parents were beside themselves, turning to everyone for help, but no one seemed to know what to do.

[1] *Nagao Kagetora is better known by his later name Uesugi Kenshin. In the traditional arrangement of the Ashikaga shogunate, Kagetora was a vassal of Uesugi Norimasa.*

Hidetsuna spotted a Buddhist monk in the crowd, borrowed his robe, put it on, and had his head shaved by Toyogorō. He then had two riceballs prepared and, holding them in both hands, walked over to the barn—without, of course, his sword. When the madman saw him, he shouted his threat that one step inside the barn would mean the child's death. Hidetsuna held out the riceballs and calmly said to him, "I've heard you haven't eaten anything since yesterday. I have brought one riceball for the child and one for you out of the Lord Buddha's compassion." He then said he would throw the riceballs to him, rather than hand them over directly. The madman was gripping the child's neck with his left hand and holding a sword in his right hand. Hidetsuna first threw one riceball. The madman let go of the child and caught it in his left hand. Hidetsuna threw the second riceball, and the madman let go of his sword and caught the riceball in his right hand. At that instant Hidetsuna jumped into the barn, kicked the sword away, and wrestled the madman down.[2]

Seeing a swordsman deliberately drop his weapon and subjugate a wild man with an unsheathed sword, the Buddhist monk was impressed. When Hidetsuna returned the robe he had borrowed, the monk in turn presented it to him as a symbol of Hidestuna's attainment of *kenzen itchi*, the state where swordsmanship and Zen are perceived to be one.[3] Hidetsuna is said to have treasured the Buddhist robe and bequeathed it to one of his students.

The second episode concerns Hidetsuna's meeting with Yagyū Muneyoshi.

MUNEYOSHI. The oft-quoted story of this encounter tells of the astonishing ease with which Hidetsuna defeated Muneyoshi, then renowned as the best swordsman in the Kyoto region. Hidetsuna first had his student Toyogorō fight Muneyoshi. It is said that Hidetsuna cut a presentable figure, with gentlemanly bearing and sharp eyes. Toyogorō, in contrast, was skinny and scruffy. This might have annoyed the proud Muneyoshi. As it turned out, he was no match for Toyogorō, who casually beat him three times in a row. Hidetsuna then faced him; but no sooner had he said, "I'm taking your sword," than he had Muneyoshi's sword in his hand. He too beat him three times.

---

[2]*A variation of this story was used by Kurosawa Akira in one of the brilliant opening sequences in his movie* Seven Samurai.

[3]*Zen is a school of Buddhism: hence, the symbolic meaning of presenting a swordsman with a Buddhist robe.*

4   Some say these matches took three days; some, a few moments. Either way, Muneyoshi was not the sort to dwell on his injured pride. Made aware of Hidetsuna's vastly superior skill, he at once asked to be accepted as a student and offered him a horse, two kegs of wine, five bundles of seaweed, and a barrel of celebratory rice. Hidetsuna stayed with the Yagyū family during the winter that followed. In the spring came the news of his son's death in a battle, and he left. As he did so, he told Muneyoshi to master the "no-sword" technique on his own. "No-sword," or mutō, is the art of taking an opponent's sword when you don't have one.[4] In Hidetsuna's own explanation, he was once drawing ideographs on the sand in a temple garden when a madman abruptly slashed at him from behind. Hidetsuna lept aside, held with both hands the blade of the man's sword, and forced the man down. Since then he had been thinking of perfecting the art of overcoming an armed opponent unarmed, but he did not think he had acquired satisfactory skill.

Muneyoshi was more than eager to take on his teacher's assignment. He worked hard at it, and when Hidetsuna returned a year later, he was ready to show what he had learned. He asked Hidetsuna's student, Suzuki Ihaku, to be the attacker, and put away his sword. Ihaku asked if it wasn't necessary for them to reach certain understandings beforehand to avoid injury. Muneyoshi said it wasn't, for *mutō* required that attacks be sudden and unexpected. He then turned his back and started to walk away. Ihaku followed, his sword ready, but then asked aloud if the experiment wasn't wrong because Muneyoshi in fact anticipated an attack. Muneyoshi agreed and, saying they would try it all over again, started to turn about. Seizing that very moment, Ihaku attacked. His idea was to catch Muneyoshi off guard. But Muneyoshi reacted with alacrity. He dodged several quick blows and within seconds had wrested Ihaku's sword from him. Hidetsuna was amazed. After observing a whole set of *mutō* matches, he presented Muneyoshi with a certificate of the mastery of swordsmanship.[5] The certificate reads in full:

---

[4]*Yamaoka Tesshū (1836–1888), a swordsman and statesman, also advocated* mutō. *In his case, it meant forgetting the sword and concentrating on the mind. For a fuller description of the Yagyū's* mutō, *see pp. 98–100.*

[5]*Called an* inka. *Originally an* inka *was a Buddhist document certifying a student's maturity in training for enlightenment. A swordsmanship* inka *follows a certain format. Hidetsuna's, cited here, is a fairly typical example.*

You must train even harder than before.

I have had an ambition to master swordsmanship and military tactics since my childhood, and have explored the secrets and the depths of various schools. As a result of my thinking and training day and night, heaven responded kindly and I founded the Shinkage school. When I came to Kyoto in order to spread it throughout the land I unexpectedly met you, and you were solicitous and sincere in countless ways. Difficult though it is for me to express adequate gratitude for your consideration, I would like to state here that I have transmitted to you all I have learned in this one school and the state of mind to be achieved through it, leaving out nothing. Should there be any falsity in this statement, may the punishments of Marici, the Great Boddhisattva of Hachiman, the Heavenly God of Tenman, the Great Bright God of Kasuga, the [the Thunder God of] Mt Atago come down upon me! From now on, if people show a sincere interest, you may instruct them up to the "Nine Kinds"[6] with their firm pledge [to follow through]. As for anything beyond, you must choose those who are truly worthy. In the Kyoto region I have managed several hundred disciples. Such an accomplishment makes me "one man in one country." So is this certificate written.

Despite such outstanding achievement in swordsmanship, Muneyoshi, himself the head of a small military clan, went through a more complicated web of military alliances, betrayals, and disappointments than Hidetsuna. I will mention just three battles in which he fought. The first took place in early 1566, not long after Hidetsuna gave him the certificate. In this battle he struck down several enemy soldiers, a feat that earned him a letter of gratitude from his lord. But he was also wounded, his hand pierced by an arrow. Had his retainers not rushed in to protect him, he might have been killed. The second battle, in 1571, left his army trounced and his first son, Shinjirō, crippled for life. In the third, in 1577, the forces of the man he had served for years were quashed by those of Oda Nobunaga (1534–1582), by then the most powerful warlord in Japan.

Muneyoshi then withdrew to his village and evidently did not associate himself with a prominent military leader until 1594, when Tokugawa Ieyasu (1542–1616) summoned him. At the time a ranking general under Nobunaga's successor Toyotomi Hideyoshi (1542–1598), who unified Japan, Ieyasu asked to see Muneyoshi ostensibly to observe his skill in "no-sword." When Muneyoshi was ready, the general himself

[6]See pp. 31–38.

6   played the offensive role. The weaponless swordsman took away Ieyasu's sword in an instant. Ieyasu promptly submitted to Muneyoshi a *kishōmon*, or *seishi*, a written pledge to become a student.

> Sir:
>
> Re: *Kishōmon*
>
> *Item:* Transmission of the Shinkage school of swordsmanship.
> *Item:* Before receiving an *inka*, I will not tell what I have learned to anyone else, be he my parent or my child.
> *Item:* I will never show any disrespect to you.
>
> Should there be any falsity in this statement, may the deities all over Japan, great and small, and especially Marici, mete out heavenly punishment on me. Hereby so pledged:
>
> Third Year of Bunroku [1594]
>
> Third of the Fifth Month   Ieyasu (signed)
>
> To Lay Priest Yagyū Tajima

Ieyasu's true reason for summoning Muneyoshi, however, may not have been the latter's reputation and prowess as a swordsman. Dissension among Hideyoshi's top aides was increasing, and the ever wily Ieyasu was secretly reaching out for potential allies. Muneyoshi did not have a powerful army, but his territory had some strategic importance. Indeed, in 1600, when the now deceased Hideyoshi's commanders broke up into two camps, East and West, and fought in Sekigahara, Ieyasu, the leader of the Eastern group, used Munenori, Muneyoshi's fifth son,[7] as the recruiter of troops from Muneyoshi's region.

MUNENORI.   Munenori's service to Ieyasu during the battle of Sekigahara was a turning point for the Yagyū family. Just a year earlier, the seventy-year-old Muneyoshi had written a will in which he asked that if he "fell dead in some place," the income from the sale of their tea utensils be used for his "funeral and other household expenses for the time being." The Yagyū family's finances had been deteriorating since 1594, when the family's farmland was confiscated by the Toyotomi government for failing to report

---

[7]*Munenori became the family heir because the first son was incapacitated in battle, the second and third became priests, and the fourth was killed in battle.*

it properly for tax assessment. But now, for Munenori's services, the newly dominant Tokugawa restored to the family all its farmland, amounting to the annual income of 2,000 *koku*.[8] The following year Munenori was awarded an additional income of 1,000 *koku* and appointed instructor in swordsmanship for Hidetada, who was to become the second Tokugawa shogun (1578–1632; ruled 1605–1623).

Munenori's rise to prominence in the Tokugawa system thereafter was slow but steady. In 1615, during the Osaka summer campaign,[9] he upheld his honor as a bodyguard by swiftly killing seven of the enemy's special attack force that had penetrated close to Hidetada's camp.[10] In 1623 he was appointed the instructor of swordsmanship for Iemitsu, the third shogun (1604–1651; ruled 1623–1651). In 1632 his income was increased to 6,000 *koku*. Two months later he was appointed an ō-metsuke, or inspector general. The primary duty of this position was to keep an eye on daimyo—samurai with minimum holdings of 10,000 *koku*—and other important officials.[11] That same year Munenori completed his most comprehensive treatise on swordsmanship, the *Heihō Kaden Sho*.

In 1636, with his annual income raised to 10,000 *koku*, Munenori joined the prestigious ranks of daimyo. At the time of his death in 1646, his income stood at 12,500 *koku*. He is no doubt the only professional swordsman who served three shoguns, attained such a high position, and exerted the kind of influence he did at the seat of government.

As a swordsman of such importance, Munenori has a good number of stories told about him. Although most of them are the creations of storytellers of the later periods, two examples may help illustrate the kinds of things the popular mind expected of a swordsman of Munenori's rank.

[8]*One* koku *represents about five bushels of rice. One* koku *was thought to be adequate to feed an adult for a year.*

[9]*The second of the two military confrontations that Ieyasu devised to eliminate the remnants of the Toyotomi and their sympathizers. The first took place toward the end of 1614 and is known as the Osaka winter campaign.*

[10]*This is the only recorded incident where Munenori is said to have actually engaged in killing as a swordsman.*

[11]*Because of his positions as shogunal swordsmanship instructor and* ō-metsuke, *Munenori is often depicted in popular fiction as a scheming, ruthless killer agent who did not bat an eye at committing murder on his own or on command. Though he is likely to have supervised some executions, the popular image is probably inaccurate.*

8   One day in late spring, Munenori, an old man then, was standing in his garden watching cherry blossoms falling, when he sensed a sudden threat behind him. An accomplished swordsman was supposed to sense even an invisible threat, so Munenori was considerably discomfited to turn around and find only his page holding his sword reverently, as was his duty, but nothing remotely threatening. He was discouraged enough by his apparent misperception to retire to his room. Later in the evening, one of his servants noticed his master was in none too sanguine a frame of mind, and asked why. Munenori appeared relieved by this inquiry and explained what had happened earlier. Hearing the story, his page, sitting near him, fearfully volunteered a confession. When he was standing behind him in the garden, he momentarily wondered if in such a peaceful setting even a great swordsman like Munenori couldn't be off guard enough to be struck from behind. So it was the page's *thought* that Munenori perceived as a threat. This discovery restored Munenori's good humor, and the page was praised for his honesty.

The third shogun Iemitsu was fond of sword matches. Once, when he arranged to see some of his outstanding swordsmen display their skills, he spotted among the gathering a master equestrian by the name of Suwa Bunkurō, and impulsively asked him to take part. Bunkurō responded by saying that he would be pleased to if he could fight on horseback, adding that he could defeat anyone on horseback. Iemitsu was delighted to urge the swordsmen to fight Bunkurō in the style he preferred. As it turned out, Bunkurō was right in his boasting. Brandishing a sword on a prancing horse wasn't something many swordsmen were used to, and Bunkurō easily defeated everyone who dared face him on horseback. Somewhat exasperated, Iemitsu told Munenori to give it a try. Though a bystander on this occasion, Munenori at once complied and mounted a horse. As his horse trotted up to Bunkurō's, Munenori suddenly stopped his horse and slapped the nose of Bunkurō's horse with his wooden sword. Bunkurō's horse reared, and while the famed equestrian was trying to restore his balance, Munenori struck him off his horse.

Munenori and His Influence

Quite apart from such stories, Yagyū Munenori had considerable weight with the Tokugawa shogunate, and a good part of his influence undoubtedly derived from his position as the shogun's instructor of swordsmanship. Because it was the shogun's choice, the Yagyū school of swordsmanship, Shinkage, carried legitimacy and prestige. Some daimyo sought and received direct instruction from Munenori, a few becoming dedicated and superior swordsmen in the process.[12] Many others invited Munenori's top students to become their instructors.

Munenori's influence also derived from his force of character and intelligence. This is especially clear in his relation to the shogun Iemitsu. The words of Katsu Kaishū (1832–1899) are often quoted in this regard. A swordsman who in 1860 commanded the first Japanese warship to pay a courtesy call on the United States and who later became the Minister of the Navy, Kaishū said that Munenori was "no run-of-the-mill swordsman," but "had extraordinary power" over "that unruly shogun." In making this assertion, he cited Munenori's action at the Shimabara rebellion. This rebellion in Kyushu erupted toward the end of 1637 as a result of the severe taxation of the Shimabara region and the savage persecution of Christians in a region noted for prominent converts. The 37,000 rebels in an old castle kept up their resistance for more than three months, until starvation under siege and assaults by the government force of 120,000 soldiers brought them down.

In referring to Munenori's action, Kaishū is likely to have had in mind a story recorded by Arai Hakuseki (1657–1725), a Confucian scholar and close adviser to the shogun Ienobu (1662–1712; ruled 1709–1712). It is a story that deserves retelling.

On the tenth of the eleventh month, 1637, Munenori was a guest at a banquet when one of his retainers came to tell him of a Christian uprising in Kyushu and the shogun's appointment of Itakura Shigemasa as commander of the subjugating army. Quickly he borrowed a horse from his host and galloped to Shinagawa, then to Kawasaki, but at each junction he was told that Shigemasa and his troops were several miles ahead. Because the day was ending, Munenori turned back, hurried to Edo Castle, the shogunal residence, and requested an immediate audience. When Iemitsu came out to see him, Munenori said that he had tried but failed to stop Shigemasa by giving a false countermand. When asked why in the world he had done such a thing, he explained that Iemitsu had erred in appointing none too weighty an official like Shigemasa to subdue a religious uprising. He predicted that Shigemasa was doomed to failure and death.

---

[12]*Nabeshima Motoshige (1602–1654), a daimyo with holdings of 75,000* koku, *was one such swordsman. Munenori's admiration for him was high enough for him to give Motoshige the most beautifully bound edition of the* Heihō Kaden Sho *on his deathbed.*

Irked by such a blunt assessment of a measure he had just taken, Iemitsu left the room. But Munenori would not leave, so the shogun returned and demanded further explanation. Munenori's argument went like this. The "way of the warrior" is essentially based on not fearing death. But even the most competent general seldom manages to turn every one of his men into a fearless fighter. On the other hand, fervent religionists delight in dying for their faith. That is why when united in a desperate cause, they make an awesome fighting force.

Now surely Shigemasa is competent and fearless, Munenori reminded the shogun. During the winter campaign of Osaka toward the end of 1614, the then twenty-five-year-old Shigemasa was selected out of the hundreds of thousands of warriors on the Tokugawa side to take a cease-fire document to the enemy camp alone. And he carried out his mission admirably. Nevertheless, he has not held important posts since then, and with his present income of 15,000 *koku* he does not carry much weight among his peers, especially those daimyo far from the seat of government. If, as is likely, the local daimyo in the Shimabara region do not follow his orders, Iemitsu will be forced to replace him with someone more important in rank and prestige. If that happens, how can Shigemasa possibly return alive to Edo? To lose a competent warrior like Shigemasa in that fashion would be a disgrace. He, Munenori, therefore now requests official permission to recall Shigemasa. It is not too late to convince Shigemasa of the reasons for his replacement without embarrassing him.

Apparently Iemitsu was persuaded by Munenori's argument, but somehow unable to reverse himself, took no action. As it turned out, practically all of Munenori's prediction came true. The local daimyo would not follow Shigemasa's orders, and all of his attacks failed. One of the top shogunal counselors was named new commander. Informed that he was to be replaced, Shigemasa ordered a general attack to achieve his mission before the arrival of the new commander. But that too ended in failure because of the insubordination of the local daimyo. Utterly frustrated and shamed, Shigemasa scaled the rebel's castle with a small company of men and was killed.

This story may sound a little pat, as if reconstructed backward from historical facts to present Munenori as an ideal advisor, one unafraid of contradicting his master. Some say, for example, that had Munenori been serious about halting Shigemasa, he could have easily used the network of secret police—or *ninja*, if you will—under his command. But there are few reasons to doubt the plausibility of the story. For one thing, though Confucian-oriented, the narrator Hakuseki was a serious historian, and he was describing an action of someone close to the shogun Iemitsu. If he had known it was a total fabrication, he would not have told the story, which after all put Iemitsu in a poor light. For another, Iemitsu evidently was the last Tokugawa shogun to maintain close personal relations with his subordinates, and Munenori was one of his closest friends. The institutionalization of national government, which got under way during Iemitsu's rule, soon isolated the shogun. A shogun's willingness to hear out a bearer of bad tidings and the opportunities for him to do so are likely to have diminished markedly after the third shogun. But it is thought that Iemitsu himself still could and did act as a ruler able to display an appreciable amount of human sentiment.

The affinity the third shogun felt toward Munenori may be discerned from a remarkable letter he wrote to the fencing instructor. Though with no indication of the year, the letter is dated the sixth of the sixth month, and reads in full:

Item: I don't use swordsmanship to have fun or to kill time. These past few years I've been practicing it with an ever deeper sincerity, because I've found that you understand swordsmanship as a matter of how to control the mind and you handle swordsmanship at will.

Item, Just in case you think I'm practicing swordsmanship while neglecting its spirit, I am writing this and having it sent to you.

Item: Because I think that a samurai, high or low, can do nothing but grasp how to control his mind, I keep swordsmanship deep in my mind, am sincere about it, and never forget about it, morning and evening. But probably because my mind isn't up to it, I can't handle it at will.

Item: Mine, I should think, differs from the attitudes of your low-ranking students. Because I truly think of your swordsmanship as deserving sincerity, I never stop dwelling on it. For that reason I've been on friendly terms with you since I was a kid.

Item: As for my swordsmanship, you only compliment it and don't try to teach me so that I may truly improve. I don't think you are being true to yourself. Even with regular fellows you ought to be sincere in teaching. But when I am so sincere, you don't try to make me truly improve, but teach me as though it's what you have to do. I don't think you are being true to yourself.

Item: During these past years you gave me your book,[13] I gave you my *seishi,* and above all, you said you taught me everything to be learned, without exception. So I was satisfied, was always on friendly terms with you, and even allowed you to join the ranks of lords.

---

[13]*Probably something akin to the* Heihō Kaden Sho.

12   Nevertheless, because you didn't put your mind to teaching me everything to be learned, my swordsmanship isn't good at all. If, from now on, you truly think of me, decide that my swordsmanship is useless, and teach me with the utmost care, I'll be satisfied. Swordsmanship handled in regular fashion is of no benefit. Unless I can control my mind and make it follow my will, I don't think my swordsmanship has any use. Whether to make my swordsmanship better or leave it as it is, is up to you. I have itemized my thoughts so that you may understand. If even at this late date you don't tell me about swordsmanship, I would assume, as you seem to think, that it is utterly useless. Now that you know I am this sincere about swordsmanship, if you decide to let it go at that, you might as well assume that my friendship with you was for naught. If you understand this one letter, think of me, and tell me truly about swordsmanship with the utmost care, I will make arrangements so that not only you but also Samon and your other children will suffer from no shortage of means long after your death. If your children were no good, that, of course, would be a different matter.

At once threatening and solicitous, at times lordly but essentially remonstrative, this letter shows the shogun Iemitsu in awe of Munenori the swordsman, yet with a deep affection for him. The official record of the Tokugawa shogunate reports Iemitsu's frequent visits with Munenori. "Munenori is no longer with us, and my sorrows know no end"—this phrase appears in Iemitsu's letter posthumously raising the swordsman's court rank by one grade. The phrase might have been routine, but it rings true in this case.

Shinkage and the Heihō Kaden Sho

Swordsmanship as we know it seems to have emerged during Japan's Warring States period—the hundred years after the second half of the fifteenth century, when a great number of chieftains fought among themselves mainly to protect and where possible expand their domains, but also to seize hegemony over the entire nation—to become the shogun, the emperor's deputy, and to oversee the military affairs of the state.

       There were no doubt men who were adept at using the sword before that time, but they are not known to have pursued the use of the sword for its own sake. And it is a curious fact that the pursuit of swordsmanship intensified after the value of the sword as a military weapon was greatly reduced. In 1542 or 1543, the harquebus was accidentally introduced to Japan and quickly spread throughout the country. The battle of Nagashino, the 1575 confrontation between Oda Nobunaga and Takeda Katsuyori (1546–1582), the heir of the aforementioned Shingen, showed the vast superiority of the firearm. To make up for its chief drawbacks of slow loading and short range, Nobunaga had three thousand harquebusiers line up in three ranks and fire in turn in volleys. The result was the destruction of Katsuyori's finest cavalry.[14] Munenori himself curtly noted that when it comes to *uchimono*, weapons that accomplish their aim by leaving their user, "nothing bests the bow and the gun."

The Shinkage (new *kage*) school of swordmanship grew out of the Kage school, which was established by Aisu Hisatada (1452–1538). What does *kage* mean? Hisatada did not leave any word on it, but Hidetsuna, who "extracted the special subtleties" from the Kage school to found his own, suggested that *kage* meant favoring being passive over being active or aggressive. In a brief piece describing the Shinkage school that he is said to have given to Muneyoshi in 1566, he states that the school aims to "come up with a series of measures by changing in response to the opponent, just as one handles the sail by watching the wind and releases the hawk upon seeing a rabbit." Yagyū Mitsuyoshi (1607–1650), Munenori's son and a great swordsman himself, was more explicit. In his treatise *Tsuki no Sho* (Notes on the Moon), he says: "The sword of the Shinkage school is not a yang blade, but a yin (*kage*) blade; it does not employ any posture, its posture being posturelessness. The position of the Shinkage school is to do things in response to the opponent's moves. It is a school that aims not to slash, not to take, not to win, not to lose." In short, *kage* means rejection of offense in favor of defense, of outward manifestations in favor of inner workings, of the body in favor of the mind.

How did such a school gain influence in a world of physical combat where practicality should have reigned supreme? The principal reason is likely to have been the waning of the importance of one man's brawn and bravery in the face of the increasing weight of infantry in military confrontations—a process no doubt accelerated by the introduction and widespread employment of the gun during the sixteenth century. As his military significance was reduced, the professional warrior-swordsman was compelled to seek some spiritual meaning in the mastery of the sword to maintain his reason for being. The changing attitude to the sword and swordsmanship may be

---

[14]*The final sequence of Kurosawa's movie,* Kagemusha, *depicts this battle.*

illustrated by two men, Tsukahara Bokuden (1490–1571) and Yagyū Muneyoshi, who each left a set of one hundred *tanka* on being a swordsman.[15]

Bokuden's reputation as a warrior-swordsman is formidable. From 1612, when he was twenty-two, to 1662, when he was seventy-two, he took part in thirty-nine battles and fought nineteen duels outside the battlefield. The number of warriors and swordsmen he felled totaled 212. But he never lost a single match, and sustained only six arrow wounds in his lifetime. Reflecting this combat-packed life, most of Bokuden's hundred verses describe practical aspects of battle-readiness. More than a quarter of the verses are devoted to the sword; nine to the bow; seven to the horse; five to the spear; five to maneuvering in a battlefield; and so forth.[16] A handful of pieces touch on the more abstract side of being a warrior, but even the state of mind these describe is strikingly practical:

> *If in his mind the warrior doesn't forget one thing,*
> *death, he'll never find himself caught short*

> *The lesson the warrior learns in every case*
> *is ultimately, finally the one thing: death*

> *If the warrior proceeds by casting aside the two things,*
> *life and death, nothing at all can best his mind.*

Muneyoshi's battle experience is less impressive than Bokuden's, and there appears to be no record of duels with swordsmen that actually involved killing. Even so, the contrast between Bokuden's verse and Muneyoshi's[17] is immediately notable. Where Bokuden's concerns are practical, Muneyoshi's are philosophical. Muneyoshi starts off by saying:

---

[15]Tanka *is a poetic form consisting of 5, 7, 5, 7, 7 syllables. Composing a set of one hundred* tanka *was begun by the court poets, but nonpoets also frequently used the format to express their thoughts. I am indebted to Imamura Yoshio for my analysis of the two sets of didactic verses.*

[16]*Because this verse set, while mostly concerned with weapons and fighting, does not mention the gun, it is thought that Bokuden wrote it before the middle of the sixteenth century.*

[17]*Actually the set contains 102 tanka, of which 10 are by a different person.*

Having no means of crossing this life,
I make swordsmanship my hiding place, sadly relying on it

15

Good to make it a hiding place—
swordsmanship has no use for fighting over things

Though I may win in sword fights,
I'm a stone boat unable to cross the sea called life[18]

After denigrating swordsmanship in this fashion, Muneyoshi goes on to argue that swordsmanship is meant for disciplining oneself and attaining virtues which in the end might help keep the world peaceful.

In swordsmanship, always train and discipline yourself,
but don't show it—hide it, be modest about it

If your mind reaches the ultimate of swordsmanship,
the sword and other implements will have no place

In swordsmanship, never let yourself go, be attentive,
and don't say too many words that prick up somebody's ear

If ultimately able to do with no sword,
a swordsman has no use for the sword on his hip

The ultimate of swordsmanship lies in the Five Virtues[19]—
keep this always in the depths of your mind

Swordsmanship is for yourself in impossible situations—
keep this in mind and train hard

[18]*A pun on Sekishūsai, another name of Muneyoshi. Sekishū means "stone boat."*
[19]*The five virtues in Confucianism: humanity, loyalty, courtesy, wisdom, and trust.*

If you become a teacher of swordsmanship,
first teach your student the laws and look into his mind

If you aren't modest but show off your swordsmanship,
you'll be hated by people and be embarrassed

When you count all the benefits of swordsmanship,
there are so many, encompassing the virtues of heaven and earth

Among those who control the world and protect the state
there's no one who doesn't employ swordsmanship in his mind

The historic shift from practicality to philosophical speculation apparent in the two warrior-swordsmen, Tsukahara Bokuden and Yagyū Muneyoshi, was carried over to Muneyoshi's son, Munenori, and the emphasis on mind over body became central to the *Heihō Kaden Sho*, the most important of all the writings about the Shinkage school of swordsmanship.

Generally, the philosophical underpinnings of the emphasis on the mind can be traced to the Buddhist postulate that "there are no particular Laws in the Three Worlds; everything is the doing of a single mind." The related position of the *Heihō Kaden Sho* that the ideal mind might be achieved through swordsmanship derives from Buddhist, Confucian, and Taoist philosophies, which suggest implicitly or explicitly that the pursuit of any worthy endeavor leads to spiritual liberation. The pursuit can be anything: dancing, garden designing, tea drinking, sword brandishing. Once something is taken up and becomes a serious undertaking, it is called *michi* or *dō* (*tao* in Chinese), "the Way." And mastering the Way means becoming enlightened.

More specifically, the emphasis on the mind in the *Heihō Kaden Sho* was a result of Muneori's association with Takuan (1573–1645), a distinguished Zen master of the Rinzai sect. Zen took root in Japan in the thirteenth century and strongly influenced the military class, which had recently gained power and was to run the country until the middle of the nineteenth century. Zen is thought to have had a special appeal to the warrior because of its stress on a highly regulated way of life, simplicity, discipline, and the equation of life and death. Of the two Zen sects that survived and gained prestige, Rinzai, founded by Eisai (1141–1215), aimed to achieve enlightenment mainly through intuition, while Sōtō, founded by Dōgen (1200–1253), did so through a concentrated pursuit of an ascetic daily routine.

Zen as understood by Munenori, however, carries Takuan's personal imprint. It is not known when the swordsman first met the Zen man, but they seem to have become close friends about the time Takuan was embroiled in a religious argument with the Tokugawa government, and exiled, in 1629. When Takuan was pardoned on the second shogun Hidetada's death in 1632, Munenori introduced him to the third shogun Iemitsu, who developed an extraordinary attachment to the monk and had a temple built for him. For some time, Takuan lived with Munenori.

Of Takuan's two treatises on Zen and swordsmanship, the *Fudōchi Shinmyō Roku* (Divine Record of Immovable Wisdom) is thought to be the first of its kind and was widely regarded as a bible by practitioners of the martial arts during the Tokugawa period. It is usually assumed that Takuan wrote it for Munenori; one text even ends with several paragraphs admonishing the swordsman on his indulgent social behavior. There is the possibility, however, that it was prepared at the request of the shogun Iemitsu, who later gave it to Munenori. In any event, Takuan's thesis on the supremacy of the mind is indelibly impressed upon Munenori's book. The origin of the other treatise, the *Taia Ki* (On the T'ai-a), is less certain, and its content more general. But there is no doubt that this short piece too helped promote the notion of *kenzen itchi,* "Swordsmanship and Zen are one."[20]

Zen as described by Takuan essentially is a means of achieving a perfectly contained but totally liberated mind. In the *Fudōchi Shinmyō Roku*, Takuan describes the ideal mind by first explaining the term *fudōchi*, "immovable wisdom":

> *Fudō* [immovable] does not mean the immobility of a stone or a tree. The mind which moves over there, to the left, to the right, in the ten directions and in the eight directions, but does not tarry anywhere for a second, has *fudōchi*....Likewise, the Fudō Myō-ō [Immovable Bright King—Japanese name for Acala] symbolizes the human mind that does not move, the body that does not unsettle. Not unsettling means not staying with anything.[21]

---

[20]To complement Munenori's Heihō Kaden Sho, *I have translated excerpts from Takuan's two books. The portions not translated in the* Fudōchi *are those that are repetitious, plus the paragraphs admonishing Munenori. As for the* Taia Ki, *only the parts written in Chinese are rendered into English. The book consists of several paragraphs in Chinese, each followed by an extensive commentary in Japanese. Takuan may or may not have written the commentaries.*

[21]See p. 3.

18   He also refers to a phrase used by the Chinese philosopher Mencius, "Seek the released mind," and explains:

> What [seeking the released mind] means is that you must search and seek the mind that has been released and bring it back to yourself. For example, if your dog, cat, or chicken is released and goes off some place, you will search and seek it and bring it home....Nevertheless, a man by the name of Shao K'ang Chieh said, "You must release your mind." This is just the reverse. What he means is that if you keep your mind in leash, it will become exhausted and won't work like a cat, and that therefore, lest your mind stay with you and become tainted, you must use it well, leave it alone, and chase it off, wherever it may be.[22]

Or, using a more graphic image:

> If you put an empty gourd on the water and touch it, it will slip to one side. No matter how you try, it won't stay in one spot. The mind of someone who has reached the ultimate state does not stay with anything, even for a second. It is like an empty gourd on the water that is pushed around.[23]

The *Heihō Kaden Sho* details from various angles how essential it is for the swordsman to train himself so that he may have such a mind.

With its stress on the mind and its predilection for philosophizing and abstraction, the *Heihō Kaden Sho* is in stark contrast with the *Gorin no Sho* (A Book of Five Rings) by Munenori's contemporary, Miyamoto Musashi (1584–1645).[24] At the outset of his treatise, completed in 1645, Musashi vows not to use "ancient words and phrases of Buddhism and Confucianism" in presenting his view, and indeed he does not. The *Gorin no Sho* is a straightforward description of the practical aspects of fighting with weapons, mainly swords. It is not that Musashi was not interested in attaining "the Way." By his own account, he gave up fighting in his late twenties after defeating all of his opponents in each of more than sixty duels. Thereafter he concentrated on "gaining a deeper principle," and when he was about fifty he saw the light. The pursuit of

---

[22]*See p. 119.*

[23]*See p. 118.*

[24]A Book of Five Rings: Miyamoto Musashi, *tr. Victor Harris. New York: Overlook Press, 1974.*

swordsmanship as a means of reaching a higher awareness was a matter of great concern to Musashi, as it was to Munenori.[25]

The difference between the two swordsmen may derive, in part, from the difference between their social positions. Munenori was a shogunal counselor who counted among his friends daimyo, nobles, monks, and artists. Musashi, not quite unlike Tsukahara Bokuden, was an independent operator who lived by the sword. More to the point, however, the difference may come from the fact that Musashi's sword was meant to kill, whereas Munenori's was not. Hidetsuna, the founder of the Shinkage school, devised the *fukuro-shinai*, a sword made of bamboo and leather. Compared with the wooden sword, let alone the real sword, the *fukuro-shinai* vastly reduced injury upon impact. In addition, the "fighting" of the Shinkage school under normal circumstances was intended only to show *kata*, forms.[26]

Hidetsuna, Myneyoshi, Munenori, and Mitsuyoshi were evidently superior swordsmen, although Mitsuyoshi reports the complaint of some contemporary swordsmen that because of the school's emphasis on formal training and on the mind, "Shinkage declined in quality from the time of Lord Munenori." Even so, the idea of *mutō*, fighting an armed opponent when you are unarmed, which the Shinkage school held to be its ultimate goal, was largely a result of its rejection in principle of destruction of the opponent. In that sense, the Shinkage school of swordsmanship was pacifist.

[25] *Various movie versions of the life of Miyamoto Musashi present him as a seeker of the Way.*

[26] *Among Muneyoshi's set of* tanka, *from which some were quoted earlier, is this piece:*

> *This swordsmanship we learn directly with our live bodies*
> *is quite different from the matches with real blades*

Heihō Kaden Sho

音六多仏云應作女
善観美
澤廬建妙老幸後筆

Family-Transmitted Book on Swordsmanship

Volume One

The Shoe-Offering Bridge[1]

[The original title of this volume, *Shinrikyō*, refers to an anecdote of the early Han dynasty (206 B.C.–A.D. 220), as told by the historian Ssu-ma Ch'ien (145?–90? B.C.). Once an old man, while crossing an earthen bridge, dropped his shoe under the bridge; thereupon a young man who happened by quickly retrieved it for him. As it turned out, the old man was the famous recluse Huang-shih Kung. Touched by the young man's behavior, he taught the youth, Chang Liang, the art of war as developed by the sage Lü Shang, of the eleventh century B.C., who is said to have guided the mythological sage king Wen in military matters. Chang later used that knowledge in helping Liu Pang (247–195 B.C.) pacify the land and found the Han dynasty as Emperor Kao-Tsu.]

[1] *This volume, in the original, consists mainly of a listing of posturing instructions and the names of fighting tecniques developed by the Shinkage school. My translation incorporates the pictorial catalogue of fighting techniques known as* Shinkage-ryū Heihō Mokuroku, *which Yagyū Muneyoshi gave to the Nō actor Komparu Ujikatsu in 1601. The accompanying descriptions in the catalogue were written by the swordsman Matsudaira Nobusada in 1707 at the request of descendants of Ujikatsu. My explanation in English of each fighting technique blends Nobusada's description and the description by Sano Masahisa in the* Yagyū-ryū Shin-hishō, *which he published in 1716. Masahisa studied swordsmanship under Yagyū Muneari, Munenori's grandson.*

The Book of the Shinkage School of Swordsmanship

THE THREE ELEMENTS[1]

- Posture
- Arms and legs
- Sword

Begin your study with the three items listed above; they are the gate for the beginner.[2] Along with the three elements, learn the following five points [instructions on posture when facing an opponent]:

- Hold your body sideways to your opponent.
- Regard your opponent's fists as equal to your shoulders.
- Make a shield of your fists.
- Stretch out your left elbow.
- Put your weight on the forward knee and stretch out your rear knee.

The points above describe the initial posture.

---

[1] The original for "three elements," sangaku (three learnings), refers to kai-jō-e, the three basic stages of study a Buddhist monk is required to work through toward enlightenment. Kai is observance of precepts set up for discipline; jō is mental concentration for achieving a Zen state; and e is awakening to the wisdom of the Lord Buddha.

Though here the term is used rather mechanically, sangaku carries special weight in Zen. For example, Chūgan Engetsu (1300–1375), a Japanese Zen monk, said: "Rectifying oneself by being sincere inside—this is jō. Jō is evidenced by quietness. When there is quietness, there is truthfulness. Without truthfulness there cannot possibly be jō. When it manifests itself outwardly as action, it is called kai. Kai is not doing forbidden things. When something is forbidden, respect comes into being. Without respect, there cannot possibly be any rule of conduct. If you teach others with an awareness of this, they will obey and follow you. That is called e. E is born of brightness. Brightness is born of wisdom. Without wisdom, there cannot possibly be e."

[2] Allusion to a passage in the Chinese classic Great Learning: "Master Ch'eng I said, 'Great Learning is a book left by the Confucian school and is the gate that the beginner enters to gain virtues.'"

The initial posture is called *the wheel.* It is the way you hold your sword. Because you can rotate your sword, we have named it the wheel. Hold your sword sideways. Let your opponent cut toward your left shoulder and as he does so, rotate your sword and win. Keep your posture low.[1]

In general, your posture is intended to prevent your opponent from slashing you. It is like setting up a castle and digging a moat to hold your enemy off. It is not meant to slash your opponent. Don't attack casually, but hold yourself carefully lest your opponent slash you. For these reasons, this is the posture you must learn first.

---

[1]*See the fighting technique* Ittō ryōdan, *p. 24.*

26   THE FIRST FIVE[1]

Ittō Ryōdan: Splitting the opponent in two with a stingle stroke

As elsewhere, the opponent is depicted at left. You face the opponent sideways, holding your sword on your right, downward, the sword tip facing away from you. When the opponent swings his sword down at your left shoulder, swing your sword up and, in a semi-circle (the wheel), strike his fists. As you do this, your left shoulder will twist away from its original position and escape the enemy sword.

Because of the low posture you assume, this technique is nicknamed *chinryū,* "a dragon crouching in the water."

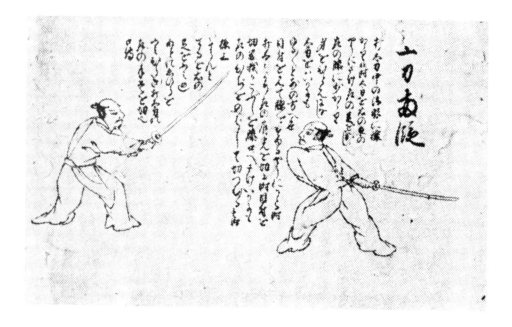

---

[1]*These are called* sangaku *techniques and are all* tai *or "waiting" stances. For* tai, *see the section on* ken-tai, pp. 63–66. *The names of the five techniques appear in the Zen classic* Hekiganroku *(Blue Cliff Records), but the meanings of the original phrases may have only accidental relevance.*

Zantei Setsutetsu: Cutting through nails, severing steel 27

When the opponent holds his sword directly in front, like a shield, cross your sword with his at the ridgeline a few inches from the tip. When he tries to push your sword aside, give in, then swiftly swing it into his right arm with all your might. Or, the moment he strikes at your right shoulder, step forward with your left leg and strike his fists or arm. Then if he swings his sword up for a second strike, strike his left wrist with an upswing.

Hankai Hankō: Turning halfway, facing halfway

28

When the opponent, holding his sword somewhat to the right, strikes at your fists, you dodge the strike by moving your sword and yourself to the opponent's right. Then, when he swings his sword up, step in and strike his left wrist.

Usen Saten: Wheeling right, turning left *29*

A technique in close, quick combat. The moment the opponent strikes at your left arm, you slip to the left under the sword and strike his right arm. Or, the moment he strikes at your right arm, you step to the right and strike his arm.

Chōtan Ichimi: Long and short are one

When your opponent is a little too far from you and continues to assess your moves but does not strike, seize an appropriate opportunity to lower your sword, hold it below your belly, and put your left shoulder forward. The moment your opponent strikes at the shoulder, thrust your sword forward with full force and defeat him.

THE NINE KINDS[1]

Hisshō: Sure victory

You hold your sword in a yin position—over the right shoulder, the blade inclining upward and back. When the opponent strikes at your fists with a downswing, you strike the enemy sword aside with a downswing, and as he lifts his sword for a second blow, you strike his hands with an upswing.

---

[1]*These are the combat techniques Hidetsuna selected from the various schools of swordsmanship of the time and improved upon. Mitsuyoshi characterized these as backup methods to be employed when you miss on the first strike. Masahisa described them as techniques for tempting the opponent to make a move so that you may make your own decisive move.*

32 *Gyakufū:* **Cross Wind**

You hold your sword in a yin position, quickly move to the left side of your opponent, and give a downswing strike. The moment he dodges, you position your sword to your left and, as he lifts his sword, strike his hands. Or, when the opponent strikes with a downswing, you hit the sword aside and, with a reverse swing, strike his right arm.

The name of this technique may derive from the swirling movement of the sword.

Jūtachi: Cross-shaped sword   *33*

When you decide that parrying with your opponent is leading nowhere, you seize
an opportune moment to lower your sword to your navel and hold it horizontally,
directly in front, the left leg forward. The moment he steps forward, you do the same;
and as he strikes, you strike his right wrist or fists with an upswing. If the opponent
does not come forward but strikes with a downswing from the initial position, you lift
your sword and strike his arms with a slanting downswing.

The name of this technique may derive from the approximate cross shape that
the extension of your sword makes with the hilt of the enemy sword when you are
holding your sword at the navel position.

34 · *Kaboku:* Softening

When the opponent holds his sword in front, facing you directly, and does not make a move, step forward and touch his sword with yours from the right side, a few inches from the tip. The moment he moves forward in response, step aside to the right and strike his fists.

Shōkei: Shortcut

This is a technique to be employed in a narrow space like an alley where the brandishing of long swords is difficult. When the opponent strikes from a yin position, you stop it by holding your sword by the hilt with the left hand and by the ridgeline with your right hand. Then you push the enemy sword up and push yours down on him, or thrust your sword forward into him from the point where you have stopped his downswing strike.

This technique is said to require the kind of mental preparedness needed when you do not carry a sword (see the section on "No-sword," p. 98–100).

Kozume: Delicate parrying

You hold your sword in a yin position, or over your head. When the opponent moves forward, put your right leg a little backward, and the moment he strikes, step forward and strike his arms.

Ōzume: Large-scale parrying

When the opponent holds his sword as you do, directly in front, seize an opportunity, strike forward toward his face, and smash his fists. Or, when the opponent moves forward, lift your sword a little and strike.

Unless the timing is perfect, this technique is likely to end up with the opponent hitting you at the same moment you hit him—a situation to be avoided.

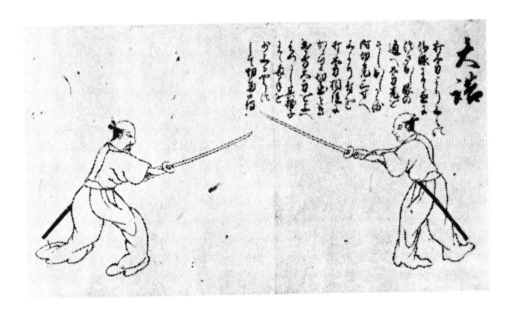

38   *Yaegaki:* Eightfold or double fence

When the opponent holds his sword low at the right knee, you also lower your sword and touch the enemy sword with yours a few inches from the tip. The moment the opponent tries to push your sword aside, thrust yours forward into his chest.

This is called "pushing into a lion's den."

Murakumo: **Rising cloud**

When either combatant's moves are leading nowhere, seize an opportunity to lower your sword to your right knee. The moment the opponent strikes at your fists, move your left leg forward, dodge his sword, and strike his arm.

40 THE GOBLIN'S SELECTION:[1] EIGHT IN ALL

Kasha (also known as *Kōrinbō*): Flower wheel

When the opponent cuts at you with a downswing, block his sword with yours, bring your right foot forward, and cut at him. As he steps forward to strike, dodge to the left, bring your right foot forward, and strike his fists.

Or, when the opponent takes a waiting stance, positioning his sword in no specific way, move forward within striking distance and hold up your sword to the right. The moment he strikes at your left shoulder, strike back and win.

[1] *These are attack maneuvers. According to Mitsuyoshi, they are based on double-dealing and essentially follow your opponent's moves and changes.*

Tengu, here translated "goblin," is, as the illustrations show, an imaginary creature combining human and crow forms, and is said to be able to fly and to possess other superhuman abilities. Legend has it that when he was a boy, Minamoto no Yoshitsune (1159–1189), an outstanding military commander, learned combat techniques and military maneuvers from the tengu inhabiting Mt. Kurama in Kyoto.

Akemi (also known as *Fūgenbō*): Open body

While parrying, you move forward to feign attack and touch the opponent's sword with yours a few inches from the tip. As the opponent bites the bait and strikes at your fists, dodge instantly and strike his fists. Or, the moment the opponent tries to push your sword aside with his, step in and strike his arm.

42 **_Zentai_ (also known as _Tarōbō_): Waiting fully**

When the opponent strikes at your fists from a midposition, block his sword with yours from above. As he tries to pull his sword down in order to strike at your elbow with an upswing, push your sword forward forcefully and strike his fists.

Tebiki (also known as *Eiibō*): Entrapment   *43*

When parrying appears to be leading nowhere, feign sudden withdrawal by lowering your fists. The moment the opponent takes the bait and strikes at your fists, quickly reverse the positions of your feet, forward and backward, jerk your fists to the right to dodge the coming blow, and strike his fists.

Ranken (also known as *Shutokubō*): Wild sword

You attack the opponent's right side, moving your left leg rightward and holding your body sideways. As you strike at his sword with yours held in one hand, he pulls his up, then strikes at your left shoulder. As this happens, you strike his sword with an upswing, and holding your sword with both hands, strike his fists.

THE SWORD AND THE MIND

Jo (also known as *Nigusoku* and *Chiraten*):[1] Introduction

This is a technique to combat an opponent with two swords. When the opponent faces you with his two swords crossed in front of him, you strike at the cross section to assess his next move. If he lowers his left sword and strikes at you with his right, you move your left foot outward and strike his right fist, instantly switching your attention to the opponent's left sword. The moment he attacks you with that sword, strike his left fist.

No one can use two swords simultaneously. But two swords can be implemented in quick succession, and from the outset you must be wary of tricky moves the opponent might make.

Nigusoku, another name for this technique, means "two instruments."

---

[1]Jo, ha, kyū, *the names of this and the two techniques which follow (and used for other things as well), are dance music terms that originated in China. The founder of the Nō theater, Zeami (1363–1443/45), used this concept extensively and argued that the three movements of introduction, development, and finale could be applied to the arrangement of plays for a day-long performance, as well as to the performance of the briefest musical note. The concept of jo-ha-kyū has also been adopted in many other fields, such as* kemari *(football) and* renga (linked verse).

Ha (also known as *Uchimono* and *Karanbō*): Development

This is another technique for combatting an opponent with two swords. When the opponent strikes at you with the sword in his left hand, you move your right foot to the right and strike that sword down. As the opponent strikes at your fists with his right sword, turn back and strike his fist.

From the outset you must know that the first attack the opponent makes with his left sword is meant to distract you, but you must not rivet your attention on that fact. Instead, you must deal with each move quickly, as it comes.

Kyū (also known as *Futarikake* and *Konpirabō*): Finale 47

A technique to combat two opponents—one to your right, the other to your left. The moment you block the sword of the first attacker, you switch your attention to the other opponent; the moment the second one strikes at you, you must switch your attention to the first one. That is the principle. In an actual combat, you must deal with the two opponents in quick succession, with powerful strikes, in the manner of the *Gyakufū* (cross wind) technique.

When you face three opponents simultaneously, the assault from the one in the middle will be difficult to deal with. So you move quickly either to the left or to the right of the group, so that you can confront a single opponent at a time, with the moves of the other two blocked by that person. The same principle applies when you face four or more opponents simultaneously. The important thing is to remain close to or within striking distance of the immediate opponent you are to dispose of. If you remove yourself from striking distance, you will put yourself in danger of being surrounded by others.

Futarikake, another name for this technique, means "two persons attacking."

SUPREME MANEUVERS: SIX IN ALL[1]

Tensetsu Ransetsu: Close slashing, wild slashing

You hold your body sideways, positioning your sword above your head fluidly, with the left hand holding the forward part of the grip of the sword. The moment the opponent strikes at you with a downswing, swirl your sword down to strike his wrists. If he brushes your sword aside, continue your upswing and downswing swirls until you win.

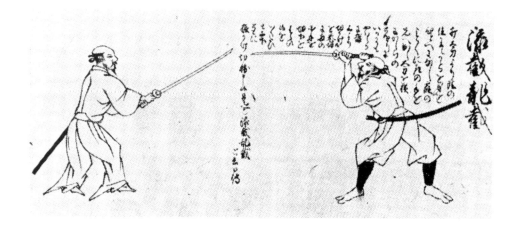

[1] *These six are the ultimate maneuvers in the Shinkage school of swordsmanship. In Muneyoshi's catalogue,* tensetsu *and* ransetsu *are lumped together, and* kōjo *is added before* gokui. *Mitsuyoshi explains: "With* muniken *you defeat someone who confronts you with the* tensetsu-ransetsu *posture; you defeat* muniken *with* katsuninken, *defeat* katsuninken *with* kōjō, *defeat* kōjō *with* gokui, *and defeat* gokui *with* shinmyōken, *which is the ultimate.* Shinmyōken *is so called to indicate that there is nothing beyond it."* Shinmyōken *is a technique of overpowering the opponent without injuring him with the sword.*

Muneyoshi's catalogue illustrates only three of these techniques: tensetsu-ransetsu, muniken, *and* katsunintō *(the same as* katsuninken *), and provides only verbal descriptions for* jōjō, gokui, *and* shinmyōken. *The catalogue mentions eight additional maneuvers called* hisshō *(sure victories),*

Gokui: Mastery

When the opponent, holding his sword directly in front, swiftly and relentlessly moves toward you, hold your sword downward to your right, dodge his advance by quickly moving your right foot outward, and as he passes by you, strike him from behind. [No illustration.]

Muniken: Incomparable sword

When the opponent faces you in the *tensetsu-ransetsu* posture, you hold your sword in a low position, with the right foot forward and the left foot backward, stretched out. The moment he strikes down at you, strike him with an upswing.

but neither illustrates nor describes them. According to Masahisa, they are sarutobi (monkey flying), tsubame-mawashi (swallow turning), tsukikage (moon and darkness), yamakage (mountain and darkness), uranami (bay waves), ukifune (floating boat), sekkō (helmet breaking), and tōbō (sword and stick).

Masahisa says the goal of the Shinkage school is to "slash the skin and flesh, but not to hurt the bones." It aims primarily for "winning over the two fists—disabling the opponent by hitting his fists.

Katsuninken: Life-giving sword[1]

When the opponent positions his right leg forward with his sword lowered, you assume the same posture and assess his moves and the striking distance. The moment he strikes, step forward, strike back, and win.

---

[1] *The term, along with* setsunintō *(death-dealing blade), appears several times in the* Hekiganroku. Katsuninken *is also used as the heading of Volume Three, and* Setsunintō *as that of Volume Two.*

Shinmyōken: Divine sword

When the opponent assumes the *Katsuninken* posture, do the same and move forward to attack. When he tries to dodge, move up to him, lay your sword across his chest, put your left leg between his legs, and by pushing your knee against his, force him down. [No illustration.]

Learn all these maneuvers thoroughly, so that you may begin devising hundreds and thousands of maneuvers. "Three Elements," "Nine Kinds," and the like are no more than generalizations. After mastering this art, you must not talk about such things as the number of combat maneuvers.

Plotting Stratagems within the Tents

"By plotting stratagems within the tents for encampment, he ensured a victory a thousand miles away."[1]

What this means is that by plotting various stratagems beforehand, you can defeat an enemy a thousand miles away before you ever meet him on the field. If you are willing to apply this observation to swordsmanship, regard your mind as the tents of the encampment. If you keep your mind alert, watch your opponent's moves and actions, and variously try double-dealing on him to see how he reacts, you may regard this as "plotting stratagems within the tents." And if you observe well how your opponent reacts and then defeat him with your sword, you may regard this as "assuring a victory a thousand miles away." Winning a battle by commanding a great army should be no different from winning a sword fight in a one-to-one combat. Win a battle involving great armies the way you win a cutting match involving two swords, and win in a stratagem for a cutting match the way you win a battle involving great armies. Winning or losing by the sword depends on the mind. It is with the mind that you move your arms and legs.

---

[1] *Passage from* The History of the Former Han, *completed by Pan Ku (A.D. 32–92).*

52 *Jo, Ha, Kyū*

Jo, ha, and kyū[1] consist of a total of twenty-seven fighting *(kiriai)*[2] portions:

• Jo:	Jōdan (3)	*Chūdan* (3)	*Gedan* (3)[3]
• Ha:	Jōdan (3)	*Chūdan* (3)	*Gedan* (3)[4]
		[or *Tōbō*	*Kiriai*[5]	*Sekkō*]
• Kyū:	Jōdan (3)	*Chūdan* (3)	*Gedan* (3)
		Each section in single beat[6]	

---

[1]*See note on p. 44. Mitsuyoshi says: "In attacking too, there are jo, ha, and* kyū. Jo *is before you attack.* Ha *is while you are attacking.* Kyū *is while your sword is exchanging blows with the enemy sword." In other words, each of the three sword positions [jōdan, etc.; see below] in each of the three combat techniques consists of* jo, ha, *and* kyū, *making a total of twenty-seven portions.*

[2]*Fighting with real swords, rather than* fukuro-shinai *in exercises.*

[3]*Jōdan, chūdan, and gedan are sword positions at the beginning of a combat. Jōdan is the sword held with hands positioned in front at the level of your head, the sword tilting upward toward its tip; or with hands positioned above your head, the cutting edge of the sword turned up, its tip tilting away from the enemy. Chūdan is the sword held directly forward, in hands positioned at the level of the navel. Gedan is the sword held low, its tip downward.*

[4]*Muneyoshi's catalogue presents* ha *differently:* 'Sekkō (2), Tōbō (3), Uchiai (4)." *Sekkō is a sideward blow at the enemy's neck. Tōbō is striking the left arm of the opponent when he tries to hold his sword horizontally, supporting the ridgeline with his left hand. See note on p. 000. Uchiai is exchanging blows.*

[5]*Same as* uchiai.

[6]*"Beat" as used in music or dance. In one Nō text, the dancer is instructed to "do a sequence of three steps in single beat."*

This volume is to be taught and learned by teacher and student in actual exercises, and need not be detailed in writing. For someone who has mastered the combat
maneuvers listed here, copy this volume and give the copy to him as proof that he is a
student of this school.

I have written this for my descendants.

Kamiizumi, Governor of Musashi,

Fujiwara Hidetsuna

The Late Father Yagyū, Governor of Tajima,

Taira Muneyoshi

His Son Yagyū, Governor of Taijima,

Taira Munenori

The reason I call this volume "The Shoe-Offering Bridge" is that Chang Liang
once retrieved a shoe for Huang-shih Kung and was taught the art of war as a reward.
Later, through the strategy Chang Liang learned, Emperor Kao-tsu gained control of the
land and established the Han dynasty, which lasted for four hundred years. Accordingly, I have taken the essence of the story and called this "The Shoe-Offering Bridge."
The road of swordsmanship is to be traversed using this volume as a bridge.

Volume Two

The Death-Dealing Blade[1]

Weapons Are Unfortunate Instruments

Here's what was said in the past: "Weapons are unfortunate instruments. Heaven's Way hates them. Using them when there is no other choice—that is Heaven's Way."[2]

Suppose you ask how this is so. What the statement says is that the bow and arrows, the sword, and the halberd are weapons, and that they are ominous, unfortunate instruments. Whereas Heaven's Way is the way to keep things alive, these choose to kill, and in this they are indeed unfortunate instruments. In other words, Heaven's Way hates them because they go against it.

[1]*See note p. 50.*

[2]*Allusion to Section 31 of Lao Tzu: "Good weapons are unfortunate instruments. People hate them. So someone with Tao does not rely on them…. Weapons are unfortunate instruments, and not the wise man's instruments. When he uses them because there is no other choice, he stresses straightforwardness and, in victory, does not praise himself."*

But the statement says killing man by using a weapon when there is no other choice is also Heaven's Way. Suppose you ask what the point of this is. Even though in the spring winds flowers bloom and the green increases, when the autumn frost comes, leaves fall and trees wither. This is the judgment of Heaven's Way. There is logic in striking down something when it has peaked. When someone rides his luck and does evil, you strike him down when his evils have peaked. In that sense, using weapons is said to be also Heaven's Way. At times, because of one man's evil, thousands of people suffer. So you kill that one man in order to let the thousands live. Here, truly, the blade that deals death could be the sword that gives life.

Strategies: Small and Large

There are ways of using weapons. If you don't know how to use them, you will be killed while meaning to kill. When you think of it, among the military strategies the one that entails two swords as you confront someone means only one loser and one winner. This is strategy on an extremely small scale. Winning or losing will involve little gain or loss.

When a single man wins and the state wins, and when a single man loses and the state loses, that is strategy on a large scale. Here, a single man means the general; the state, the various armies under his command. The various armies are the general's arms and legs. Making the various forces work well means making the general's arms and legs work well. For the various forces not to work is for the generl's arms and legs not to work. When you and someone confront each other with swords, you win by making your arms and legs work at will. Likewise, a general wins a battle by using his forces and by plotting well.

Governance and Swordsmanship

A man in the position of general must be able to set up camp and maneuver his army for battle not only on the actual battlefield where victory or defeat is decided, but also within the confines of his mind. The latter is the art of war in the mind.

Not ignoring a disturbance when governance is good is the basis of the art of war; so is foreseeing a disturbance from the various developments in the state and stopping it before it breaks out. When the country is governed well, it is also part of military strategy to appoint this man to this governorship, that man to that mayorality, and to give attention to the remotest corners of the land to strengthen the defense of the state. Schemes of a governor, mayor, magistrate, or village head for personal gain will mean hardship for the governed and spell the beginning of the collapse of the state.

The ability to understand this and to plot to prevent the personal schemes of a governor, mayor, magistrate, or village head from ruining the land is comparable to the ability to judge your opponent's stratagems by observing his moves in a sword fight. You must be attentive and observant. Something of greater utility can be learned from swordsmanship.

Serving Your Lord

Your lord may be flanked by sycophants, who when facing him feign an air of morality, but who when looking down at the ruled give an angry glance. Such men, unless you lie low before them, will speak ill of you for something good you have done. As a result, the innocent suffer and the sinful thrive. Understanding this is more important than the ability to judge your opponent's stratagems in a sword fight.

The state is your lord's; so are the people. Those who serve in his vicinity are his subjects, just as those who serve him in the distance. Closeness or distance scarcely matters. For the lord, his subjects are his arms and legs; the legs may be a little distant, but they are no different from the arms. Because they feel pain the same way, the arms and the legs are neither closer nor remoter. When such is the case, if those who are close exploit those who are distant, those who are distant will suffer despite their innocence and resent their lord, who should come under no such cloud.

Those close to the lord are few—five to ten at the most. Those distant are many. Those who are many will turn away from him if they resent him. Those few and close, who from the beginning think only of themselves and not of their lord, and serve him in a way that makes the people resent him, in an emergency will vie in turning away from him. When that happens, who will think of the lord? His aides are responsible for such a development; he is not to blame. It is hoped that this will be understood, and that those in the distance will not be placed outside the lord's benevolence. To grasp this truth under any circumstance is in itself part of military strategy.

Strategic Thinking in Everything

Whether a friendship remains unchanged or not from beginning to end also depends on grasping the truth, and so requires something not unlike strategic thinking. Even companionship during a gathering relies on timely judgment and therefore a strategic mind. If you fail to grasp truth, you may stay too long when you should not and end up being blamed for something groundlessly; or you may speak out without reading the workings of someone else's mind, thereby inviting a quarrel and in the end ruining yourself. All this depends on whether you grasp the truth or not.

Arranging various things in your living room through selection of an appropriate spot for each piece also requires incisive judgment of the room. Here again, something not unlike strategic thinking is needed. No matter what the subject, there is one truth, and it would do no wrong to apply that to government.

It is a prejudice to think that swordsmanship is meant solely to slash an opponent. It is meant not to slash an opponent, but to kill evil. It is a way of allowing ten thousand men to live by killing a single evil man.

What is recorded in these three volumes may not go out of this house. But that is not to make this school of swordsmanship a secret. This record is made for transmission to those who are worthy of it.[1] Without transmission, these volumes might as well not exist. May my descendants keep this in mind.[2]

---

[1] *The original is cryptic, and the translation is a paraphrase. Like any self-respecting school in many fields of endeavor, the Yagyū family used to give a certificate known as an* inka *to a student who was judged to have reached a certain level of technical mastery. For a sample, see the Introduction, p. 5.*

[2] *Here ends Munenori's attempt to explain the broad applicability of swordsmanship.*

The Great Learning *Is the Gate for the Beginner*[1]

To reach a house, you must first enter the gate. The gate is a pathway leading to the house. After passing through the gate, you enter the house and meet its master. Learning is the gate to reaching the Way. After passing through this gate, you reach the Way. Learning is the gate, not the house. Don't mistake the gate for the house. The house is located farther inside, after the gate is passed. Because learning is the gate, don't think that the books you read are the Way. Books are a gate for reaching the Way.

There are those who remain in the dark about the Way, no matter how much they study, no matter how many ideographs they learn. They may read the classics as easily as if they were paraphrases by ancient scholars, but because they are in the dark about the truth, they cannot make the Way their own. Even so, it is difficult to reach the Way without learning. At the same time, someone who has studied hard and talks smoothly may not necessarily be someone who has illuminated the Way. But again, there are those who naturally live according to the Way without studying anything.

Exhaust All Knowledge and Master Everything[2]

The *Great Learning* says: "Exhaust all knowledge and master everything." Exhausting all knowledge means knowing everything that is generally known in society and the principle of everything that exists, leaving nothing unknown. Mastering everything means that when you have come to know the principle of everything, there is nothing you don't know, nothing you can't do. When you have exhausted things to know, you have mastered all the things to do. If you have not, you cannot do anything.

[1] See note 2. p. 24.

[2] Section 2, Great Learning. *The original phrase is said to have fifty to sixty different interpretations.*

60   While you don't know about something, you have doubts about it. Because you are doubtful, that something does not leave your mind. If the principle of that something becomes clear, nothing will remain in your mind. This is what is meant by exhausting all knowledge and mastering everything.

When nothing remains in your mind, everything becomes easy to do. You learn the Way of everything in order to brush aside whatever may be in your mind. At first, because you know nothing, you do not have doubts or any such thing in your mind. Only after you begin learning do things come into your head that prevent you from doing anything with ease.[1] When the things you have learned leave your mind completely, forms and the like disappear; and as you perform each skill in your own field, it becomes easy regardless of the form. Without violating the form, you perform it unconsciously, correctly.

The same holds true in swordsmanship. Training after you have learned a hundred sword positions, after thoroughly learning whatever body position, eye position, or form there may be, is training in a state where you have exhausted all knowledge. When you have exhausted all the forms and all those forms cease to exist in your mind—that is the state where you have mastered everything. When you have exhausted all the various forms and piled up accomplishments through training and practice, movements come to exist in your arms, legs, and body, not in your mind; and whatever you do you do freely, in disregard of the forms, but not violating them. When you reach that point, you do not know where your mind is—even the Demon of Heaven or a heretic won't be able to pinpoint its whereabouts.[2] The forms exist for reaching that state. When you have acquired them, they cease to exist.

That is the ultimate end of all disciplines. The final state of any discipline is where you forget what you have learned, discard your mind, and accomplish whatever you set out to do without being aware of it yourself. You begin by learning and reach the point where learning does not exist.

---

[1] *See Takuan's* Fudōchi, *p. 112.*
[2] *See Takuan's* Taia, *p. 124.*

The Mind and the Spirit

That part of the mental makeup positioned inside to develop detailed plans is called the mind, and that part that carries out those plans, the spirit. The mind may be compared to the master, and the spirit to his servant. The mind stays inside and uses the spirit. If the spirit becomes overworked, it may stumble. You must have the spirit tethered to the mind so that it may not be carried away.

In swordsmanship terms, the firming up of your body below the waist may be said to be the mind, and the actual exchange of blows after the fight has begun, the spirit. Keep the spirit under the tight control of your body below the waist. Don't allow it to take an impetuous attack stance. It is vital to maintain calm by having the mind pull back the spirit and by not allowing it to be dragged along by the spirit.

Double-Dealing[1]

Double-dealing is the basis of swordsmanship. By double-dealing, I mean the stratagem of obtaining truth through deception. If you sense your opponent's double-dealing but still attack, you will be tricked and lose. If it is your double-dealing and you attack and he is tricked, lead him on to win. If you find out that he won't be tricked, make another attack. Then your opponent's not having been tricked will be the same as his having been tricked.

In Buddhism this is called a parable.[2] Even if you inwardly hide the truth and outwardly carry out your stratagem, when you succeed in the end in pulling your opponent into the truthful way, all deceptions become truths. In Shintoism, this is called a mystery, and by virtue of being hidden, it causes people to have faith. When one believes, there are benefits. In the military family, this is called strategy. Even

[1]Hyōri: *heads-tails, front-back, double-talk, deception.*

[2]*Originally a Buddhist term:* upāyakauśalya. *Used in the title of Chapter 2 of the* Lotus Sutra, *the word is also translated "means" or "expedient devices."*

though stratagems are deceptions, when through a deception you win without harming your opponent, the deception in the end becomes a truth. This is what is meant by "Disturb to gain peace."[1]

Beat the Grass and Surprise the Snake

"Beat the grass and surprise the snake"—so holds a Zen saying.[2] Just as you surprise the snake by beating the grass in which he lies, your scheme should be to surprise your opponent once and then surprise him again. Doing to him something he may not dream of your doing is double-dealing, or swordsmanship. Surprised, his fighting spirit taken away, he may forget his defense. Raising your fan[3] or raising your hand, may also take away his fighting spirit. Casually tossing away the sword you hold is also part of swordsmanship. If you have attained the "no-sword" state,[4] you won't be concerned with the sword. Your opponent's sword then will be your sword. This is how "seizing the chance ahead of time" works.

Seizing the Chance Ahead of Time

You may ask what I mean by "seizing the chance ahead of time." This means "before your opponent gets his chance." "Chance" here is the same as "mind"[5]—the mind he

[1] *The origin of this phrase is unknown.*

[2] *In Zen the expression means to harm one thing in order to warn and safeguard another.*

[3] *A fan was always part of a gentleman's outfit, no matter what the occasion.*

[4] *See the section beginning on p. 98.*

[5] *"Chance" and "mind" here are homophones.*

keeps to himself. Seizing the chance ahead of time means carefully observing your opponent's mind and making an appropriate move just before he makes up his mind. As the term "Zen chance" shows, this is frequently done in Zen.

63

"Chance" is the mind that is hidden and not revealed. It may be compared to the *kururu,* the device for opening and shutting the door attached on the inside. Making a move by carefully observing the chance hidden inside, not revealed, and hard to see, is called the stratagem of seizing the chance ahead of time.

Ken-Tai: *Attack Stance and Waiting Stance*

Ken is an instantaneous assault you make singlemindedly, strongly, the moment the fight begins, so as to give the first blow. The *ken* state of mind is the same whether it's with you or with the opponent. *Tai* is to hold back, without striking at once, and to wait for your opponent to attack. This requires putting yourself strictly on guard. Thus the term *ken-tai* means both attacking and waiting.

The principle of *ken-tai* exists in your body and your sword. You might throw your body near your opponent while holding back your sword. By making bait of your body so that the opponent may strike first, you win. Here, your body is in a *ken* stance, your sword in a *tai* stance. The purpose of putting your body in a *ken* stance is to force your opponent to strike the first blow.

Ken-tai exits in your mind and your body. Put your mind in a waiting stance, your body in an attack stance. If your mind takes an attack stance, it will run ahead of everything and do no good. So you must hold your mind back and win by putting your body in an attack stance and making your opponent strike first. If your mind takes an attack stance, you will first try to slash your opponent—a sure way to lose. On the other hand, it is equally possible to put your mind in an attack stance and your body in a waiting stance. This way you can make your mind work alertly and force your opponent to move first by holding your sword back. In all this, take the "body" to mean the hands that hold the sword.

Ken-tai goes both ways, but what the two ultimately mean is the same thing. What is important is to win by having your opponent make the first strike.

WHAT TO DO WHEN THE OPPONENT TAKES AN ATTACK STANCE

Note the following three points on your opponent:

- His fists
- That part of each of his arms which is folded or stretched
- His chest, especially between the shoulders

The details of these are to be explained orally.

Be prepared to take either of the following two stances, which entail your posture and sword position:

- "Distant and close beat."
  [*Mitsuyoshi:* "This stance is employed against someone who pushes in single-mindedly or attacks suddenly, powerfully. So as not to clash with that kind of extreme aggressiveness, you keep yourself in an open stance and win."]
- "Armor plate."[1]
  [*Mitsuyoshi:* "An attempt to prevent your opponent from striking you at the same time you strike him."]

The following five points concern your body and your sword. Each of them must be learned in actual exercises, for they are difficult to explain in writing:

- Making a shield of your fists
- Holding your body sideways to your opponent
- Regarding your opponent's fists as equal to your shoulders
- Holding your rear leg in an open stance
- Holding your sword exactly as your opponent holds his

You must take care, before facing your opponent, to put much thought into the setup of your body below the waist and to make yourself alert, lest you fluster after the

---

[1]Sendan, *the original word for "armor plate," appears to mean sandalwood and obliquely refers to a proverb: "The sandalwood is fragrant from the moment of bifurcation." But the intent of the reference is unclear.*

fight is on. This is vital. If you face your opponent carelessly without mental prepara-
tion, you won't even be able to employ basic forms.

WHAT TO DO IN FACING AN OPPONENT IN A WAITING STANCE

- His fists
- That part of each of his arms which is folded or stretched
- His chest, especially between the shoulders

Any of these three marking points may not be missed on an opponent firmly in a
waiting stance. Still, these points are to be noted both in attack and waiting stances, and
are vital. In making a strike, give special attention to the opponent's arms; in exchanging blows or in close combat, to his chest. Under normal circumstances, the fists are
the marking point you must not take your eyes off.

THREE TRICKS

Tsuke, kake, narai no kakari—any of these three feints may be tried to provoke your
opponent when his planned moves are hard to fathom. Try to find out his intentions.
Work any of these tricks and their subtle variations, as well as double-dealing, on an
opponent firmly ensconced in a waiting stance. Force him to make a move, and win.

FOLLOW A CHANGE, OBEY A CHANGE[1]

An opponent in a waiting stance is bound to evince some change if you show a variety
of changes yourself. Following that change, you win.

---

[1] *The original term for "change" is* iro *(color). Mitsuyoshi explains it this way:* 'Iro *refers to that
moment in the mental state of your opponent when he changes his intention—to take an attack
initiative, to get out of something, or make a switch.... The mental ability to follow an* iro *cannot
be achieved unless you attain the state where you do not assert yourself at all, but leave everything to
your opponent."*

PRETEND NOT TO SEE

While trying a variety of double-dealing tricks on an opponent in a waiting stance, you watch his moves; but as you do, you pretend not to, and as you pretend not to, you watch. Ever alert, you do not fix your eye on one spot, but move it constantly, observing what you must in glances. A Chinese poem has a line: "Pretending not to notice, a dragonfly escapes a shrike." Likewise you must constantly glance at your opponent's moves while making your own alert moves. The Sarugaku branch of Nō drama has a technique known as *futame zukai*, "using two glances." In it, the actor gives a single glance and looks away; he does not keep on looking.

Be Struck to Win

If your opponent wants to strike, let him; be struck, then win.

It is easy to give your opponent a single slash. What is difficult is not to be slashed by your opponent. Even if the opponent strikes thinking to slash you, you do not have to be surprised but can let him, as long as you are aware that the striking distance is great enough.[1] The opponent may think he can strike you but won't be able to, because of the distance. The sword that doesn't hit is a dead sword. At once you jump forward, strike, and win. The opponent's first strike misses, enabling you to get your first into him. After your first strike, you musn't even allow him to lift his hands. Should you hesitate after you've struck, your opponent's second strike would get you. A lapse at this moment means defeat. If your mind tarries where you've struck,[2] you'll be struck by your opponent—making your first strike useless. As long as you have struck, pay no attention to whether or not you have slashed him. Strike the second, third, then the fourth and fifth times. Do not allow your opponent even to raise his face. Winning is decided by the first strike.

[1]*See "three inches" on p. 68 and "three feet" on p. 69.*
[2]*See Takuan, p. 111.*

Three Types of Beat[1]

You and your opponent striking each other simultaneously[2]—that is one kind of beat. Striking the opponent from below as he raises his sword—that is another. Striking the opponent from above as he lowers his sword—that is still another.

We consider being in tune bad, being out of tune good. When you and your opponent are in tune with each other, he can use his sword better; when you are not, he can't. You must strike in such a way as to make it hard for your opponent to use his sword well. From below or from above, you must strike without keeping time with your opponent. In most cases, allowing yourself to be in tune with your opponent is no good.

Slow Beat versus Quick Beat; Quick Beat versus Slow Beat[3]

If the opponent moves his sword in a slow beat, you must move yours in a quick beat. If the opponent uses a quick beat, you must move your sword in a slow beat. Here again, you must use your sword so that you will be out of tune with your opponent. If you allow yourself to be in tune, the opponent will be able to use his sword well.

An accomplished Nō chanter chants off beat, so that an inexpert drummer cannot play the drum well as accompaniment. If an accomplished chanter is coupled with an inexpert drummer, or an accomplished drummer with an inexpert chanter, it should be difficult to chant or play the drum. When the same is done in a sword fight, it is called the art of slow beat versus quick beat, quick beat versus slow beat.

[1]*As in music.*

[2]*This is "abhorred" in the Shinkage school.*

[3]*Mitsuyoshi says: "Slow beat is striking with a big swing, with a shout. . . . Quick beat refers to swift, detailed moves."*

When an unaccomplished chanter chants slowly, an accomplished drummer will not be able to play the drum quickly, however lighthearted he may try to be. Again, when an accomplished chanter chants lightheartedly, an unaccomplished drummer will be left behind, unable to play the drum.

An accomplished bird-spearer[1] shows the bird his spear from a good distance, making it sway gently, and when close, quickly slides up to the bird and catches it. The bird, enchanted by the swaying rhythm of the spear, flutters and flutters his wings, trying to fly away, but unable to do so, ends up caught. The point is to stay out of tune with your opponent. Out of tune, you can step in.[2] You must contemplate even things like these.

Understanding the Startup Rhythm

In dancing or in chanting, if the performer doesn't know the startup rhythm, accompanying him will be impossible. In swordsmanship, too, there is something like a startup rhythm. You must correctly grasp how your opponent may use his sword and what tactics he may employ in order to see his ultimate intention. When you do, you are like a Nō dancer or chanter who is well acquainted with the startup rhythm. Once you know your opponent's moves and behavior well, you can work on him freely.

Six Approaches

- Strike back as the opponent strikes.
- A difference of three inches.
  [*Mitsuyoshi:* "When two combatants face each other with swords crossed, the victory is said to be with the one who manages to move his sword forward three inches ahead of the other."]

[1]Torisashi: *someone who catches birds with a pole with birdlime at its tip.*
[2]*Part of the original sentence is unclear.*

- Steal within a distance equal to the opponent's height.[1]
- Mark the opponent's elbows when he holds his sword in the upper position.
- When a "wheeling" move[2] is employed, mark that part of the sword grip between the two fists holding it.
- A distance of three feet.

    [*Mitsuyoshi:* "You must concentrate on moving close to your opponent so that the distance between the tip of your forward foot and that of his is three feet or less. . . . . If it is farther than three feet, you won't be able to strike your opponent with your sword."]

These six approaches must be learned and explained orally in actual exercises with your master. So they are not detailed in writing.

If, despite your initial feints and double-dealing, your opponent remains unalarmed and sticks to his waiting stance without making the first assault, you must steal within the three-foot distance and move close to your opponent. Then, when he cannot contain himself any longer but takes an attack stance, allow him to make the first strike, and while he is doing so, strike him. Unless your opponent strikes first, you will not be able to win. And unless you learn not to receive a hit when your opponent strikes, you cannot allow him to strike at you. You must train hard to master these things so that you may fearlessly move close to your opponent, have him strike at you, and win. This is the attitude known as *sen-sen* (initiatives above all)."[3]

---

[1] *See* suigetsu, *p. 84.*

[2] *See the fighting technique* ittō ryōdan, *for example.*

[3] *Mitsuyoshi: "My father said that this is what winning is all about, the ultimate in swordsmanship. All the various forms to be learned are meant to reach this point. If you reach this point, all the forms cease to exist. . . . If you engage in combat by placing your mind in the opponent's [i.e., you and your opponent thinking alike], the one who thinks first wins. . . . You get the first thought first, and you win a sen-sen victory. . . . Because the mind is the source of all thoughts, it comes first (sen). The first thought precedes (sen) a move. Hence, sen-sen."*

Four Other Approaches

- *Taikyoku,* or "great deception,"[1] along with "initial moves." To be orally transmitted.
- *Zanshin,* or "maintaining presence of mind at all times." Applicable in both *ken* and *tai* stances.[2] To be orally transmitted.
- Dodging the short sword by a foot and five inches.[3]
- *Ken-tai* in taking an initiative. Remember to hold your body in an attack position, your sword in a waiting position.[4]

Not one of these can be mastered without having it explained in actual exercises with your master. These approaches are difficult to describe in writing.

Listening to the Sound of the Wind and Water

Whatever else may be said, the point of swordsmanship is to win—with double-dealing as a base—by trying various moves and by constantly changing, thereby making the opponent strike first. Before the combat begins, you must assume that the opponent will take an attack stance, and you should never allow yourself to be off guard. It is of vital importance to ready the lower half of your body.

If you are not even ready to think that the opponent will take an attack stance and if, the moment the fight begins, you are attacked sharply in a rapid succession of moves, you will not be able to make any move, let alone use what you have learned in daily exercises. After combat begins, it is vital to keep your mind, body, and legs in an attack stance, and your hands in a waiting stance. Give special attention to the movement of your opponent's eyes. It is even said that you must make it your own. Unless

[1]*Mitsuyoshi explains that* kyoku, deception, *is a technique of winning that lures the opponent to strike first by showing an apparent weakness.*

[2]*See pp. 63–66.*

[3]*The "foot and five inches" refers to the width of the shoulders, but the meaning of the phrase is not clear.*

[4]*See pp. 63.*

you can follow your opponent's eye movement with absolute calm, whatever you may
have learned about sword handling will be of no use.

Listening to the sound of the wind and water means maintaining a calm surface
and a fighting spirit within.[1] The wind itself has no voice; it makes a sound only when it
strikes something. As it blows high above, it is quiet. When it touches trees, bamboo,
and a thousand other things down below, its voice comes forth, noisy, busy. The water
too, as it begins to fall from above, has no voice. When it touches something below and
settles, it speaks with a busy voice. With these as metaphor, we say, "Maintain a calm
surface and a fighting spirit within." This is to be apparently quiet, unfluttered, and
calm on the outside and to keep a fighting, alert mind on the inside.

It is bad to have a busy body and limbs. The *ken-tai* stances must be maintained
inside and outside. It is bad to have only one or the other stance. Try to keep up a
mental state where yin and yang constantly appear by turns. Movement is yang; calm is
yin. Yin and yang must separately manifest themselves, inside and outside. If yang
moves inside, the outside must be yin and calm. If the inside is yin, movement appears
outside. Likewise, in swordsmanship, you make your mind work, move, and be alert,
while keeping your body unfluttered and calm outside. This yang movement inside
and yin calm outside follows Heaven's principle. Also, if the outside is in a sharp attack
stance, an attempt must be made to keep the mind inside from being carried away by
the outside; for if the inside is kept calm when the outside is in an attack stance, the
outside will not be confused. If both the outside and the inside move, there will be
confusion. Make the outside and the inside differ from each other: *ken* versus *tai*,
movement versus calm.

Just as a waterfowl afloat on the water maintains an outward calm while using its
webbed feet busily below, so must the mind inside be kept on guard. And if you
continue your training in this fashion, the mind inside and the outside will melt into
one, and the distinction between the two will disappear. To attain that state is the
ultimate of the ultimate.

[1]*Mitsuyoshi gives a different interpretation of the phrase "listening to the sound of the wind and
water." "This teaching," he says, "is meant to suggest that before you reach the three-foot distance
from your opponent, you must maintain an absolutely calm state of mind where you can hear a
faint breath of wind or listen to the soft purling of water flowing." Elsewhere, he cites 5-7-5-syllable
verses to describe the requisite state of mind before two swords meet:*

A flower scattering falls on the moss with no sound

A flower scattering can be heard in these mountain depths

Diseases

It is a disease to be obsessed by the thought of winning. It is also a disease to be obsessed by the thought of employing your swordsmanship. So it is to be obsessed by the thought of using everything you have learned, and to be obsessed by the thought of attacking. It is also a disease to be obsessed and stuck with the thought of ridding yourself of any of these diseases. A disease here is an obsessed mind that dwells on one thing. Because all these diseases are in your mind, you must get rid of them to put your mind in order.

Two Stages of Getting Rid of Diseases

THE INITIAL STAGE[1]

"A wish occurs and ceases to exist. An attachment occurs and ceases to exist."[2] This observation may be explained this way:

The thought of ridding oneself of a disease is a wish. When the thought occurs, a wish occurs. The disease here is a singleminded, obsessive wish. The thought of ridding oneself of a disease is also a wish. Therefore, one gets rid of a wish with a wish. When a wish is gotten rid of, it ceases to exist. Hence: "A wish occurs and ceases to exist."

If the disease remaining in a wish is gotten rid of with a wish, then both the wish to get rid of the disease and the wish to be rid of it cease to exist. The same thing is meant by the saying, "Remove a wedge with a wedge." When a wedge cannot be pulled out, you can pull it out by hammering another alongside it, thereby loosening it.

1,3*The original words for "initial stage" and "final stage" are Zen terms indicating stages of training.*

2*A Zen saying said to have been cited by Takuan.*

When the first wedge is pulled out, the second one that was hammered in will not be left. Similarly, when a disease is gotten rid of, the wish to get rid of the disease will not be left. Hence the observation above. Further, the wish to rid oneself of a disease is something that grows in attachment to the disease, but if the disease is gotten rid of along with that attachment, the attachment will not be left. Hence the observation, "An attachment occurs and ceases to exist."

THE FINAL STAGE[3]

In the final stage, the state of having no thought whatsoever of ridding oneself of a disease helps get rid of it. The thought of ridding oneself of a disease is a disease. When you manage to leave yourself to a disease and stay in the thick of it, you have already gotten rid of it. You think of ridding yourself of a disease because it has not been gotten rid of but remains in your mind. In that state, the disease is not gotten rid of, and whatever you do or think remains attached to something and results in no benefits.

How shall I understand this matter? I asked. In reply, he said: I have set up the two stages, initial and final, for a purpose.[1] If you train and continue to train to achieve the state of mind of the initial stage, any attachment will leave you on its own without your trying to get rid of it. A disease is an attachment. In Buddhism, attachment is abhorred. A monk who has left all attachments may mingle with the worldly, but will remain unaffected. He does whatever he pleases with utter freedom. And he is correct in any move he makes. Experts in various arts and skills may not be called masters (*meijin*) as long as they remain attached to what they do. An unpolished jewel attracts dirt and dust. A polished one doesn't become soiled even if put in the mud. Train hard and polish your mind so that it may remain unsoiled. Leave yourself to a disease and abandon your mind so that you may do whatever you please.

---

[1] *It is thought that Munenori asked the question and Takuan answered it.*

The Mind in a Natural State

74

A monk asked an ancient man of virtue,[1] "What is the Way?" The man of virtue said in reply, "The mind in a natural state is the Way."[2]

This story contains a principle that applies to all arts. It puts forth the ultimate truth. A natural state of the mind is one in which all the diseases are eliminated and you mingle with diseases and do not have them. Let us apply the principle to some actual arts. If you are conscious of shooting an arrow when you are doing so, you will not be able to take aim properly. If you are conscious of using a sword when you are doing so, you will not be able to hold steady the tip of your sword. If you are conscious of writing something when you are doing so, you will not be able to handle your brush properly. When you play the *koto*, if you are conscious of it, the music will be out of tune. Someone who shoots an arrow must forget that he is shooting an arrow; if he shoots an arrow with the same state of mind as when he is doing nothing, he should be able to take aim properly. Using a sword, riding a horse, or whatever—do it with a natural mind such as that when you are not using the sword, not riding a horse, not writing, not playing the koto, not doing anything at all. Then everything will be done without difficulty, smoothly, with ease.

[1] *Ma-tsu Tao-i (709–788), with whom Zen is said to have made its real start in China. More than 130 of those who studied with him went on to become eminent Zen masters. According to legend, he "had an imposing appearance, with piercing eyes, and is said to have looked like a tiger and walked like a bull. He could stretch out his tongue so far that it covered his nose."*

[2] *In a fuller context: "The Way does not use training. Simply avoid becoming polluted. What is pollution? To make something, to work for some goal, only with life and death in mind, is all pollution. Should you want to understand the Way at once, you must know that the mind in a natural state is the Way. The mind in a natural state has neither the intention to make something nor the intention to distinguish right and wrong, neither selectiveness nor interruption of normalcy, neither ordinariness nor holiness."*

This appears in the Keitoku Dentō Roku *(Ching-te ch'uan-teng lu, or* Transmission of the Lamp; *circa 1007), one of the documents recording famous Zen masters' words and deeds. The postulate, "The mind in a natural state is the Way," is further expounded in Soku 19 of the Zen classic* Mumonkan.

The Keitoku Dentō Roku *also has a passage: "A monk asked, 'Why is it that you say, "The mind is the Buddha?" ' The master [Ma-tsu] said, 'To make an infant stop crying.' The monk said,*

In whatever art you pursue the Way, if you are singleminded and determined to accomplish what you set out to, you are no longer pursuing the Way. Someone with nothing in his mind is a man of the Way. If you have nothing in your mind, you can easily do whatever you do. A mirror, always clear, with no form or shape of its own, distinctly reflects whatever faces it. The mind of a man of the Way is like a mirror; because it has nothing and is clear, it is "mindless," and is lacking in nothing. That is the mind in a natural state. Someone who does everything with his mind in a natural state is called a master.

No matter what you do, if you do it singlemindedly, trying to control your mind correctly and not allowing it to be distracted, you will end up becoming muddle-headed. You do something right once, so you think you are good enough; but then you do it wrong. You do it right twice and wrong once, so you may be pleased that you have reached a point where you do something right two out of three times; but then you do it wrong twice in a row and find everything confusing. All this is because you are determined to do something well.

Still, in time your achievements add up, and as your training continues, the mind set to do well what is being done will recede into the distance, and whatever you do, you will do without thinking, without intending, regardless of yourself, just like a wooden puppet.[3] That is when you are not aware of yourself, and your arms and legs do whatever they are supposed to without your mind contriving things—that is when you do right whatever you do ten out of ten times. Even then, if you allow your mind to interfere if only slightly, you will miss it. If you are "mindless," you hit it every time. "Mindlessness" does not mean having no mind whatsoever; it simply means the mind in a natural state.

'What will you do if the infant stops crying?' The master said, 'Neither the mind nor the Buddha.' "
The two pronouncements, "The mind is the Buddha" and "Neither the mind nor the Buddha," pro-
vide the bases for Soku 30 and 33 of the Mumonkan. See also Soku 3, 53, 73, of the Hekiganroku.
[3] The correct meaning of the original word for "wooden puppet," dōkō no bō, appears to be "beginning puppeteer."

Be Like a Wooden Figure

"Like a wooden figure facing flowers and birds" are the words of Layman P'ang.[1] A human figure made of wood does not become affected mentally even if its eyes apparently see a flower or a bird.[2] A wooden figure has no mind and therefore cannot be affected—quite a logical thought. How can a human being with a mind be like a wooden figure? A wooden figure is a metaphor. A man with mental faculties cannot be equated with a piece of wood; he cannot be like bamboo or a tree.

What is meant is that when you look at a flower, you must not do so with the renewed realization that you are looking at a flower. You must look with a natural mind, "mindlessly." When you shoot an arrow, you should not do so with the renewed realization that you are shooting an arrow. You must shoot an arrow with a natural mind. A natural state of the mind is the state of mindlessness. If you change the natural state of the mind and allow a new mind to come into being, your mind takes on a new form and you become unsettled both inside and outside. If you do anything with an agitated mind, nothing will be done the way it should. To respond without becoming agitated by any question[3] is thought praiseworthy. I must note especially that all the buddhas are said to have immovable minds.[4]

These two points[5] apply in the effort in swordsmanship to rid the mind of diseases.

Release the Mind

Chung-feng[6] said: "Be equipped with a mind that releases itself."[7] There are initial and final stages in doing so.

[1]*Successor of Ma-tsu Tao-i (see note 1, p. 74). He appears in Soku 42 of the* Hekiganroku.

[2]*Flowers and birds are symbols of natural phenomena that move the human heart.*

[3]*In a Zen mondō (question and answer) session.*

[4]*See* Fudōchi, *p. 112.*

[5]*I.e., "The mind in a natural state" and "Be like a wooden figure."*

[6]*Chinese Zen monk (1263–1323). He didn't settle anywhere, declining even the imperial summons, until at his followers' urging he agreed to live in a temple.*

[7]*The word* hōshin *(Chinese,* fang-hsin *), "to release the mind" or "the released mind," appears to*

If you release your mind, it will stay where it reaches. So, to prevent it from staying, we tell you to take it back, to bring it back, where it belongs. That's the training in the initial stage. If you give a blow, your mind will stay where the blow has struck. We tell you to find it and bring it back to yourself.

In the final stage, we tell you to release your mind and let it go wherever it wants to. You release your mind after making it one that will not stay in any place even if you release it. If you have a mind that releases itself, it would be awkward to keep it in check all the time. A mind that releases itself is one that doesn't stay anywhere after it releases itself. If you are equipped with such a mind, you can work freely. With a leash in hand, you can't be free. Even dogs and cats are best kept unleashed. You can't raise a dog or a cat always on a leash.

The reader of Confucian books becomes burdened with the concept of kei[1] and, considering it indispensable to self-improvement, spends all his life bound to it. That is like keeping the mind on a leash like a cat.

Buddhism has a similar concept. A *sutra* has the term *isshin furan*, "single-minded and undistracted." This means putting your mind on a single thing and not allowing it to be distracted in other directions. There is also a phrase to be recited, "I respectfully say the name of the Lord Buddha." In *keirei*, you face a Buddhist statue and pay respect to it singlemindedly. All this has an effect not different from *kei*.

Nevertheless, here it is a means[2] of keeping the mind from being easily distracted. A well-controlled mind has no use for any means of controlling it. You recite, with your mouth, "Great Holiness the Immovable,"[3] hold your body correctly with hands joined in prayer, and contemplate the figure of the Immovable in your consciousness. When you do this, the three karma agents of body, mouth, and conscious-

---

date from the Shu ching (The Book of Documents, eighth century B.C.), and mean different things in different times. In the Shu ching, it seems to mean a willful and licentious mind. The philosopher Mencius (371–289? B.C.) says: "The road of scholarship means nothing but finding the released mind." The poet Wang Wei (701–761) has a line in his poem "At the Melon Garden": "I release my mind and look at the whole universe." See also Fudōchi, p. 112.

[1]Kei (Chinese, ching), "respect" or "reverence," a central point in Confucian ethics, was regarded as especially important in studying the Way by Confucian scholars of the Sung dynasty (960–1234). The ideograph for ching originally meant "tensing up at inadvertently touching a ram's horn."

[2]See note 2, p. 61.

[3]Acala(-nātha). A stage in the Boddhisattva's career. See Fudōchi, note 1, p. 112.

ness[1] work in equal measure, and your mind does not become distracted. This is called the "Three Mysteries[2] in equal measure." In this, it is similar to the concept of *kei*, which is true to human nature. But *kei* is a state of mind in transition, during training. If you separate your hands and stop reciting the name of the Lord Buddha, the mental image of the Buddha also goes away. Your mind returns to the state of easy distraction; it is no longer a mind always under control. Someone who has put his mind under control once and for all need not cleanse the three karma agents of body, mouth, and consciousness, and he does not become sullied even if he mingles with dust. He keeps moving all day but remains immovable, just as the moon stays where it is even while it follows the moves of hundreds and thousands of waves. This is the realm of someone who has attained the ultimate of the Buddhist Law.

I have recorded this, as suggested by my teacher of the Law.[3]

[1] *In Esoteric Buddhism, it is believed that the essential sources of actions and deeds are the body, the mouth, and conciousness.*

[2] *In Esoteric Buddhism, the Buddha's body, word, and mind, which are said to reveal the supreme truth. A mortal might be able to come close to understanding the supreme truth by concentrating his body, mouth, and conciousness on the Buddha.*

[3] *I.e., Takuan.*

Volume Three

The Life-Giving Sword[1]

Shuji Shuriken[2]

There may be a hundred combat postures, but there is only one purpose: to win
Ultimately, all this depends on *shuji shuriken.*

You may teach or learn the use of the sword in a hundred ways, in a thousand
ways, and you may be able to handle the whole array of combat postures and sword
positions. But *shuji shuriken* is central. Your opponent may manage a hundred pos-

[1] *See note on p. 50. Muneyoshi says, "In our school the sword that is positioned for attack is called the
death-dealing blade, and the sword that is not, the life-giving sword."*

[2] *According to Mitsuyoshi,* shuji *means blocking the opponent's sword with yours crosswise from what
ever position he may strike at you; it also means the spot on the chest, below the chin, where the neck
line of a Japanese coat meets and overlaps; in striking at the opponent, that is the mark to aim at.*
Shuriken *means gaining an accurate insight into the opponent's stratagems. As a combined term,*
shuji shuriken *appears to mean either the spot to mark or judging the opponent's tactics accurately.*

*The term also refers to Esoteric practices, such as "cutting the nine ideographs" (namely, recit-
ing nine magic words) for self-protection. Originally Taoist, the practice of "cutting the nine ideographs" was taken up by yin-yang practitioners, Esoteric Buddhists, Japanese swordsmen, and ninja.
Some swordsmen and ninja executed it at daybreak every day, and many did so before an actual
combat or a mission.*

tures, and you may do the same, but what ultimately determines the outcome is how you mark the *shuji shuriken*. Because it is to be secretly transmitted, we do not give the correct ideographs for the term in writing, but use ideographs that sound the same.[1]

"Being" and "Nonbeing"

"Being" and "nonbeing" opportunities.[2] Addendum: That "being" is there, and so is "nonbeing."

In the case of *shuji shuriken*, there are "being" and "nonbeing" to be learned. What shows is "being," and what hides itself is "nonbeing." The "being" that shows and the "nonbeing" that hides itself are *shuji shuriken*. It's all in the hands that grip the sword. In Buddhism they speak of "being" and "nonbeing."[3] Something similar is spoken of here.

[1]*Mitsuyoshi is more forthright and, for* shuriken, *uses ideographs that mean "seeing the stratagems." Munenori's ideographs don't mean anything.*

[2]*Mitsuyoshi: "It's a matter of how you observe. If you spot and give good attention to an unchanging point to mark, you should be able to see the opponent's changing stratagems well. By giving attention to the "nonbeing"* [*what may appear nonexistent*]*, you can see the "being"* [*what you can see*]*."*

[3]*I can cite no specific reference. But* u, *the Japanese original for the word here translated as "being," means, in Buddhism, the tenth in the twelve* nidāna *(causes, links) that bind the human to the three worlds of the past, present, and future. In one translation, the twelve* nidāna *are: (1) ignorance, (2) actions, (3) consciousness, (4) name and form (mind and body), (5) the six entrances (the six sense organs), (6) contact, (7) sensation, (8) desire, (9) clinging, (10) existence, (11) birth, and (12) old age and death.* U, *in this sense, is a state of* kleśa *where the human mind continues to be troubled by myriad things.* Vimukti *or* nirvana *is the state attained by someone who has managed to overcome the state of* kleśa.

Mu, the Japanese original for the word here translated as "nonbeing," seems not so much a Buddhist term as one of Taoism and, later, of Zen. It appears that when the Buddhist concept of sunyata *(void, emptiness) reached China in the second century, the Chinese identified it with the Taoist concept of* mu *(*wu, *in Chinese), "nothingness."*

It is possible that in speaking of "being" and "nonbeing" Munenori had in mind one of the more famous Buddhist propositions: "What is material is void; void is material."

The ordinary man sees "being," but not "nonbeing." Someone who has learned *shuji shuriken* sees "being" and "nonbeing." For him both "being" and "nonbeing" exist. When "being" is there, you strike with "being"; when "nonbeing" is there, you strike with "nonbeing." Also, you strike at "nonbeing" without waiting for "being," and you strike at "being" without waiting for "nonbeing." So we say: " 'Being' is there, and so is 'nonbeing.' "

A note to *Lao Tzu* has the phrases, "Always [there is] 'being'; always [there is] 'nonbeing.' "[1] If "being" is always there and so is "nonbeing," "being" becomes the same as "nonbeing." When it shows, "nonbeing" becomes "being." For example, when a waterfowl is floating on the water, it is a "being"; when it dives into the water, it is a "nonbeing." That means that what you regard as a "being" becomes a "nonbeing" when it hides itself. Similarly, what you regard as a "nonbeing" becomes a "being" when it shows itself. In other words, "being" or "nonbeing" depends on whether something shows or hides itself. The essence of the two is the same. So, both "being" and "nonbeing" are always there.

In Buddhism they also speak of "true being" and "true nonbeing."[2] When someone dies, a "being" hides itself. When someone is born, a "nonbeing" appears. The essence of both remains the same. There are "being" and "nonbeing" in the hands that grip the sword. This is secretly transmitted. It is called *shuji shuriken*. If you turn your palm downward, "being" hides itself. If you turn it upward, "nonbeing" appears again. Even what these words mean should be difficult to appreciate unless they are explained orally. When there is "being," you see it and strike at it. When there is "nonbeing," you see it and strike at it. That is why we say that "being" is there and so is "nonbeing." What is called "being" is "nonbeing." What is called "nonbeing" is "being." "Being" and "nonbeing" are not two separate things. If you fail to see this, you will not be able to count on a victory even if you use your sword in a hundred different ways. A hundred stratagems ultimately rest on this.

---

[1] *The "note" is not identified, but the two phrases cited are part of the opening section of the* Lao Tzu. *The section is subject to a variety of interpretations; in one translation, it reads: "The Nameless is the origin of Heaven and Earth; / the Name is the mother of all things. / Therefore let there always be non-being so we may see their subtlety, / And let there always be being so we may see their outcome."* (A Source Book in Chinese Philosophy). *The section that follows has the sentence: "Being and non-being produce each other."*

[2] *Source not identified.*

84 *Suigetsu*

Suigetsu, or the moon on the water. Addendum: Its light.

This means forging your tactics by determining the distance between you and your opponent that is needed to make it impossible for the opponent's sword to touch your body. The art of stepping within that distance surreptitiously to get close to the opponent is called "the moon on the water" because of the way the moon casts its light on the water.[1] You must set up the needed distance in your mind before the fight begins. Details about the distance are to be transmitted orally.

Shinmyōken[2]

Shinmyōken, or divine sword. Addendum: The attention to the "seat" must also be given to the body and the legs.

Shinmyōken is of ultimate importance. The body has a spot so designated.[3] In referring to your own body, the *ken* (sword) of *shinmyōken* should be understood to be the actual sword. This is because the sword doesn't leave its "seat," whether you hold it to the right or to the left. In referring to your opponent's body, the *ken* (sword) should be understood to be *ken* (observation). Observation is vital because you cut into your opponent by giving close attention to the seat of his sword. Hence, the ideographic differentiation.

[1]*Mitsuyoshi explains the term "the moon on the water" somewhat differently: "By 'the moon on the water' we mean the length of the shadow the opponent casts. If you maintain a space between you and your opponent that is equal to his height, he won't be able to strike you, we say, no matter how hard he slashes at you."*

[2]*Different from the fighting technique of the same name. See p. 51.*

[3]*Mitsuyoshi explains:* Shinmyōken *"is where the sword settles. It is the six-inch area around the navel." He adds that* shuji shuriken, suigetsu, *and* shimyōken *are the basics of swordsmanship, "from which all other schemes derive."*

Shin and Myō

Interpretations of the two ideographs, *shin and myō.*

"When *shin* exists inside, *myō* appears outside. This is called *shinmyō.*"

Take a tree. Because it has *shin* (divinity, core) inside, the flowers bloom and emit fragrance, the green rises, and the leaves and branches flourish. These outward manifestations are *myō* (subtlety, exquisiteness). The *shin* of a tree cannot be pin-pointed as such even if you split the tree; but without *shin,* neither the flowers nor the green will show on the outside. Likewise, the *shin* of a man cannot be pinpointed as such even if you tear his body asunder; but because he has *shin* inside himself, he can perform a variety of skills. Because he has *shin* installed in the seat of *shinmyōken,* a variety of *myō* appear through his hands and feet, enabling the flowers to blossom in a fight, so to speak.

For the mind, *shin* is the master. *Shin* remains inside and uses the mind outside. The mind, in turn, uses the services of the spirit *(ki).* If the mind, which uses the services of the spirit while staying abroad for *shin,* were to stay in one spot, the purpose would not be achieved. For this reason it is vital not to let the mind tarry in one place. Suppose a master sends his servant on an errand and the servant stays put at his destination; his errand won't be done. If your mind stays with an object and does not return to where it belongs, your ability as a swordsman will be compromised. Because of this, not letting your mind tarry in one place is vital not only in swordsmanship, but in everything else.[1]

Two Notes

Ridding oneself of diseases—three points.[2] Diseases of the opponent.

The initial mark.[3] Maintaining a rhythm. To be orally transmitted.

[1] See Fudōchi, *p. 111.*

[2] *Mitsuyoshi: "Once you hold a sword, you want to strike, you want to win, and you want to have a fight. These three urges are all mental failures, of which diseases are born."*

[3] *Mitsuyoshi: "It is to concentrate on the spot you mark first....It is to win without constantly chang-ing the spot to be marked."*

86   *Walking*

When you walk, it's bad to be fast or to be slow. Walking in a natural way, gliding, unthinking, is good. To be excessive or to be inadequate[1] is bad; take the middle ground. You are fast because you are alarmed, rattled. You are slow because you are daunted, afraid of your opponent. The ideal is the state where you are not upset by anything.

Thrust your fan in front of someone with his eyes open, and he will blink—that is a natural state of mind. Blinking doesn't mean the person is upset. Repeat your thrust twice, three times, to surprise him. If he doesn't blink at all, that shows he is upset. Not to blink, refraining from doing so, trying hard not to do so, means that the mind has moved out of the natural blinking state. Someone with an "immovable mind" will blink, unthinking. That is the state where you are not upset.

The point is not to lose your natural state of mind. When you try not to move, you have already moved. The logic here is that to move is not to move. Turning is the natural state of the waterwheel. If the waterwheel does not turn, it has gone against its nature. For someone to blink is natural. Not to blink shows his mind has moved. Not to change your natural state of mind and to walk as usual, gliding, is good. This is the state where you are not upset in your appearance and in your mind.

The One Principle

The "one principle":[2] A mental attitude when facing an opponent directly in front,[3] or a mental state when dealing with a spear. Caution when without a sword.

The "one principle" above is a secret term in swordsmanship. To a swordsman, anything can happen. So what is crucial is how you act when you find yourself sud-

---

[1] *Book XI, Analects: "Being excessive is the same as being inadequate."*

[2] *Elsewhere Munenori defines the term* ichiri, *the "one principle," as* seigan no kamae, *"holding the sword in midposition" when facing the opponent directly in front.*

[3] *About* kamae, *combat engagement postures, Munenori says: "Although there are a variety of* kamae…, *in our school… we don't use any other postures than right, left, and frontal."*

denly cornered and placed in an adverse situation. Carefully watching out for any such turn of events, lest you be caught off guard, is called the "one principle."

The "one principle" also applies to the caution taken when you hold your sword directly in front, very close to the opponent, or when you face your opponent with a spear "at one foot and a half."[1] It is also the sort of caution you take when you cannot retreat farther because of a wall or a fence behind you, but the opponent continues to press you. Keep in mind that what is crucial is how you act in moments of stress. When with no sword, foiling the opponent "by one foot and a half" will not be accomplished if you keep your eyes riveted to one spot or allow your mind to tarry in one spot and be off guard. To give attention to such things is described as the "one principle," and is kept secret.

The One Foot

One foot for you and for your opponent.[2] Caution to be taken both when you and your opponent have swords of the same length, and when you carry no sword.

The equipment [the sword], for either you or your opponent, can detach itself from the body by one foot. By one foot you can foil it. To get closer than this is dangerous.

The Ultimate First Sword

"Ultimate" here means the best you can do. The "first sword" does not refer to the actual sword. Your ability to observe the intention of the opponent is couched in this

---

[1] *The meaning of this phrase is not clear. It could mean "pointed at your chest."*

[2] *Mitsuyoshi: "My father said, 'This refers to the extension and contraction of the sword, which doesn't exceed one foot. Between your fists that carry the sword forward and your shinmyōken [the navel and its vicinity] there is no more than a foot. The tip of the sword too does not extend more than a foot. To keep this one foot in mind when you strike is what you try to accomplish.'"*

THE SWORD AND THE MIND

secret term. The "first sword" is crucial because your ability to see the opponent's stratagems will lead to a decisive strike. Regard that ability as the "first sword," and the ability to use your sword according to the opponent's stratagems as the "second sword." With this as the basis, use your sword in a variety of ways.

Shuriken, suigetsu, shinmyōken, diseases—these four, plus the working of your arms and legs, and that makes five. We learn this as "five insights and one observation." Seeing the *shuriken* is called "one observation." The remaining four are called insights because they take place in the mind. Seeing with your eyes is called *ken,* observation, while seeing with your mind is called *kan,* insight, which means working it out in your mind.[1] In truth, we are speaking of four insights, rather than five, but we say "five" for convenience. *Shuriken, suigetsu, shinmyōken,* diseases, body and limbs—those five. Of these, four are what you gain through the mind, and one is what you observe with the eyes.

Distinctions among Suigetsu, Shinmyōken, etc.

· *Suigetsu* concerns judging the locus of fighting.[2]
· *Shinmyōken* is judging the crucial point of the body.

[1]*On* kan, *insight, Mitsuyoshi has this to say:* 'Kan *is to listen to the mind, see with the eyes closed, see inside.* Kan *accompanies no action. Action takes place as you follow your opponent." And:* 'Kan *is not action or double-dealing, but the basis of your mental working. It is the mind that sees things at their base. You don't allow your mind to stay in one spot. If you do, it is no longer* kan.*" About* ken, *observation, he says:* 'Ken *is to see in the present. You see something with your eyes, and your mind receives it through the nerves* (me ni mite i ni tsūjite yori kokoro ni ukuru nari). *When you see with your eyes, there's bound to be some action, some outward workings. In seeing, something goes from outside to inside."*

[2]*Munenori:* "In combat there is an area where you can strike the opponent and an area where you can't. The area where you can is the suigetsu. Outside the suigetsu you can't strike the opponent. Still, it is good to harass the opponent outside the suigetsu to see what happens."

- The "body and limbs" concerns the opponent's movements and your own movements.
- Ridding oneself of diseases is meant to see the *shuriken.*

Thus, the ultimate purpose of all this is to see the *shuriken,* the stratagems, of the opponent. The distinctions among the four are general. You get rid of diseases in order to see the *shuriken.* If you don't get rid of diseases, you are bound to become their captive and fail to see what you ought to. If you fail to see what you ought to, you lose. Diseases here mean diseases of the mind. A disease of the mind is the mind's tendency to tarry in one place or another. Try not to let the mind tarry in the spot where you have struck. The point is to cast off and not cast off your mind.

Fighting

Your opponent poises his sword and the tip of his sword comes toward you; you strike as he lifts his sword.[1]

If you want to strike your opponent, let him strike at you first. The moment you succeed in having him strike at you, you have already succeeded in striking him.

Take the locus of *suigetsu.* After that, concentrate on your mind's workings. If, despite your efforts, the opponent takes it first, regard the locus taken as yours. It's the state of mind that matters: whether the opponent comes within the range of five feet or you come within the range of five feet, the distance between you and your opponent remains the same. If the other party takes the locus, leave it at that. It's bad to have a fixation about taking the locus. Keep your body light.

Both the positioning of your feet and the carriage of your body should not be disconnected from the seat of the sword.[2] Do not forget to give attention to this even before the fight begins.

---

[1]*Mitsuyoshi: "If the opponent starts out poising his sword in the lower or midposition, he must swing it up before striking; as he does, you make your sword follow, and win. It is good to do this as if you are making your whole body follow."*

[2]*Hereafter, unless otherwise noted,* shinmyōken *will be translated "the seat of the sword."*

Three Stages in Seeing the Seat of the Sword

Seeing with your mind is the basis. It is only when you see it with your mind that your eyes notice it. So the eyes follow the mind. After seeing it with the eyes, you then see it with your body and limbs. "Seeing with the body and limbs" means trying not to allow your body and limbs to be disconnected from the opponent's seat of the sword. You see with the mind so that you may see with your eyes. You see with the eyes so that you may make your hands and feet go for the opponent's seat of the sword.

The Mind and the Moon

The mind resembles the moon in the water;
the form is like the shadow in the mirror.[1]

This verse is adopted for swordsmanship because the water holds the moon's reflection, and the mirror your body's. The human mind moves to an object just as the moon does to the water.[2] It does this swiftly. Compare the seat of the sword to the water, the mind to the moon, and let the mind move to the seat of the sword. As the mind moves to the seat of the sword, so does the body. The body follows the mind.

This verse is also used to urge you to compare the mirror to the seat of the sword and to let the body, like a shadow, move to the seat of the sword. This means that you must not allow your arms and legs to be disconnected from the seat of the sword. The way the moon moves its light to the water is swift indeed. Though the moon is high up in the sky, as soon as the clouds move away, its light reaches the water. It isn't as if its light comes down from high up in the sky, slowly, step by step, to cast its reflection.

[1] *Obviously a Buddhist verse, but no specific source is identified.*

[2] *Throughout this section, a homonymic pun is used: utsuru, here translated "move," also means "reflect." So this particular sentence may also be translated, "The human mind reflects on an object just as the moon does on the water."*

Before you can bat your eyes once, the reflection is there. In other words, the human mind moves to an object as swiftly as the moon does to the water.

The observation in a Buddhist *sutra,* "The mind is as swift as the moon on the water, as the image in the mirror,"[1] does not mean that although the moon moves to the water and looks so tangible there, you can't find it when you search for it under the water. It means that the moon, from distant heaven above, without the lapse of a second, gives its reflection as it is. The same is true of the image reflected in the mirror. Whatever object faces it is there already. This is a simile for swiftness. The human mind moves to an object the same way. While you bat your eyes, your mind goes as far as Great T'ang.[2] You nod and doze, and before you know it, your dream goes to your home town a thousand miles away.[3] The way the mind moves this way was explained, they say, by the Lord Buddha, who compared it to the moon on the water and an image in a mirror.

Application of the Same Verse

The verse cited above may be applied to the *suigetsu* in swordsmanship. You should move your mind to the locus of fighting like the moon. If your mind moves, your body will follow. So, as soon as fighting begins, you should move your body to the locus of fighting as swiftly as a mirror reflects an image. Here, keep in mind that unless you maintain the lower part of your body in readiness in advance, your body won't move well. Both with the fighting locus and the seat of the sword, the point is to move your body and limbs swiftly.

[1] *Source unidentified.*

[2] *Poetic metaphor for great distance. By then some Japanese had traveled to Europe, and they were well aware of the world beyond China.*

[3] *An image common in court poetry.*

92   *Hasty Attack*

Making a hasty attack is the worst thing of all.[1] A swift attack or attacks in quick succession are acceptable only when you hold the lower part of your body well and after you have observed the situation adequately from the beginning of the fight. Not to flutter is vital.

Turning Your Mind Back

You strike your opponent and think, "I've struck," and your mind will be stuck with that thought. Because your mind does not turn back from the moment of striking, it becomes absent, and you allow your opponent the second strike, thereby compromising your success in making the first, and lose. Turning your mind back means this: If you have struck, don't leave your mind at the point where you struck; the moment you strike, turn your mind back and see how your opponent is. Your opponent, when struck, is bound to transform himself. When struck, he thinks, "What's this! I've been struck!" and may get angry. If he gets angry, he becomes resolute. If you relax at that moment, your opponent will strike you down. Regard the opponent you've struck as a furious boar.[2] Begin with the assumption that while you think, "I've struck," let your mind tarry, and ease up, your opponent, struck, musters his determination. Also, the moment he's struck, he will become alert. So, if you strike with the same mind as before, you will miss. If you miss, your opponent will take the lead and strike you.

To turn your mind back means not to let your mind tarry at the point where you've struck, but to snatch it back to yourself. It means to have your mind back and see how your opponent appears. Or else, it is that ultimate state of mind in which you do not turn your mind back, but strike at the point you've struck a second time, a third time, with no break, so that your opponent won't even be able to shake his head. This

[1] *Munenori, elsewhere: "If you suddenly attack and strike before you reach the locus of fighting, you will fail. You must receive your opponent first and, with your mind firmly in the seat of your sword, strike back from a waiting stance."*
[2] *A wounded boar is a metaphor for an uncontrollably destructive force.*

is what is meant by "without enough space of time to allow a strand of hair."[1] It means
to strike consecutively, thwack, thwack, without allowing the space of a strand of hair
between the first strike and the second. In what is known as the "law battlefield" in Zen
dialogue, a question is responded to without the interval of a strand of hair.[2] If you
extend that interval, you'll be finished. The outcome of the contest will be clear. This is
what is meant by "without enough space of time to allow a strand of hair." It means the
rapidity of your sword striking the second time, the third time, with no break.

Ikkyo, Void, and Concentrated Mind

Ikkyo means casting off a variety of things in one bundle. "A variety of things" here
means a variety of diseases. "Diseases" here means diseases of the mind. You put in
one bundle the various diseases that exist in your mind and slice it off as with a sword.
We have described those diseases in a separate volume.[3] In essence, however, the
mind that becomes stuck is diseased. In Buddhism, becoming stuck is called "attachment" and is abhorred above all else. If your mind becomes attached to something, it
fails to see what it ought to, and despite yourself you end up losing. The tarrying of the
mind is called a disease. *Ikkyo* is to make a single bundle of all such diseases and throw
it away. You cast off various diseases in a single bundle, lest you fail to see the "only
one."

Now, the "only one" *(yuiichi)* refers to the "void" *(kū)*. The void is a code word
that is to be secretly transmitted. It refers to the mind of the opponent. This is because
the mind has neither form nor color, and is void. To see the void, or the "only one,"
means to see the mind of the opponent. Buddhism is there for you to learn that the
mind is void. However, we are told that even among those who knowingly say that the
mind is void, few are enlightened.

[1] *See* Fudōchi, *p. 114.*
[2] *See* Fudōchi, *pp. 114-115.*
[3] *See p. 72.*

Bōshin, "concentrated mind," refers to the spot on which the opponent's mind is concentrated—namely, the hands gripping the sword.[1] You strike before the opponent's gripping fists move.[2] *Ikkyo* is meant to facilitate discernment of the movement before it takes place. Wipe off the hundred diseases, and don't fail to see the void. The opponent's mind is in his hands; it is concentrated in them. Striking while the hands do not move is called striking the void. The void is something that does not move. Because it has no form, it does not move. Striking the void means striking before movement occurs.

The concept of void is central to Buddhism. There are two kinds of void: false and real. The false void is the state where there is nothing. The real void is a true void—namely, the void of the mind. The mind is like a false void in its formlessness, but it is the master of the body and everything that the body does derives from it. The moves and the workings of the body[3] are the mind's doing. A mind that doesn't move is a void. A void that moves is a mind. A void moves, turns into a mind, and prompts the hands and feet to work. You are expected to strike while the fists gripping the sword still show no sign of movement. So we say, "Strike the void."

We speak of a concentrated mind, but the mind is not visible to the eye. It is called void because it is not visible, and it is called void also because it does not move. The mind is concentrated in the hands that grip the sword, but it is not visible to the eye. The point is to strike while the mind is concentrated in the hands but still shows no sign of moving. One moment we may say that the void of the mind is invisible to

[1]*Mitsuyoshi: "Father says, '[Bōshin] is an attempt to see the spot where the mind reveals itself.'" Elsewhere: "My old father says, 'Long ago, we put the length from the elbow to the fist at 1 foot and 2.4 inches, and decided that it was best to see bōshin in that length. But a bōshin is a spot where the mind reveals itself, so we shouldn't limit ourselves to that length. The true purpose of bōshin is to find a spot, in any part of the opponent's body, where his mind reveals itself when the body is apparently not moving or at work. But mostly you should pay attention to four points: the opponent's eyes, his legs, his body, and his "1 foot and 2.4 inches." In these you can discern what you want to. You tend to turn your eyes to where your mind goes, and if you want to attack, your leg moves forward. If something's on your mind, the way you hold your body constantly changes, visibly. Needless to say, the "1 foot and 2.4 inches" is one of those spots where the mind reveals itself. But wherever it does, in any part of the body, must be regarded as a bōshin.'"*

[2]*Mitsuyoshi: "The moment the opponent decides to strike, his grip on the sword will harden. As it does, the muscles of his arms become taut. Mark that moment."*

[3]*Original, "mind."*

the eye and has no substance to it. But the next moment the same void moves and
performs a variety of things, prompting the hands to pick up something, the feet to step
in a certain way, and the body to do all sorts of subtle things.

Becoming enlightened about the mind is hard to achieve by reading books;
enlightenment is also difficult to attain by listening to sermons. We are told that as in
the old days those who copy *sutras* and those who give sermons do what they do
according to convention, and that rare are those who are enlightened of the "mind of
the mind."[1]

Enlightenment and the Way

Because all the skills and rare deeds of man are the mind's doings, heaven and earth
also have a mind. It is called the mind of heaven and earth. When this mind moves, it
causes thunder and lightning, wind and rain, and with clouds changing in color
abruptly, prompts the snow and hail to scatter and the ice to fall in the burning sky,
thereby tormenting people.

The "void," when in heaven and earth, is the master of heaven and earth, and
when in the human body, the master of the human body. When you dance, it is the
master of dancing; when you perform a Nō play, the master of Nō; when you employ
swordsmanship, the master of swordsmanship; when you shoot a gun, the master of
the gun; when you shoot an arrow, the master of the arrow; and when you ride a horse,
it is the master of the horse. If this master has any personal twists, you will not be able
to ride a horse, your arrow will miss, and your gun will not hit the target. If your body
holds itself well and your mind settles in its proper place, state, or position, you should
be able to do everything freely. It is important to find such a mind, once and for all, and
become enlightened. Everyone says, "I have my mind completely open and can use it
very well." We are told, however, that rare are those who have found in a satisfactory
way the kind of mind described above.

---

[1] *The "true mind" in Buddhism.*

The signs of unenlightenment should be apparent in the person. Those who know should be able to tell. Someone who is enlightened should be correct in whatever he does or says, and in his bearing. Someone who is not correct cannot be said to be enlightened, we are told. A correct mind is called a true mind or right mind.[1] A twisted, sullied mind is called a false mind; it is also called a human mind. Someone who realizes his true mind and meets its dictates in whatever he does deserves respect.

I am not saying these things because I have mastered my own mind. I say these things even though it is difficult for me to conduct myself, move and stay still as if my mind were correct, as if I met the dictates of a correct mind. I note this because it is a state to strive for.[2] Even so, in swordsmanship it won't do not to hold your mind correctly and move your body and limbs at will. In your conduct in daily life you may not live up to the Way, but in swordsmanship it won't do to be without the attainment of the Way. You may be able to live up to the dictates of the true mind in the discipline of your choice; however, not to deviate from the true mind in whatever you do and to be masterful in disciplines other than yours is nearly impossible. Someone who comes to know other disciplines and masters them is called "an accomplished man." Someone who has mastered one skill or one art is called an expert, but hardly an accomplished man.

True and False Minds

A certain *tanka* says:

> *Your very mind is the mind that misleads your mind.*
> *Mind, do not yield your mind to the mind.*[3]

[1] *See* Fudōchi, *p. 117.*

[2] *The original for "a state to strive for" is* michi. *The same word is translated "the Way" a few sentences later and "discipline" still further on. See Introduction, p. 00.*

[3] *The original 5-7-5-7-7-syllable tanka has detailed notes incorporated within the verse. In reference to the explanations given in the paragraph that follows, the first and second minds are "false," the third, fourth, and fifth are "true," and the sixth is "false." Takuan cites this* tanka *at the end of* Fudōchi, *in a section not translated in this book.*

This *tanka* speaks of truth and falsehood. There are two kinds of mind: true and false. If you realize your true mind and do things accordingly, whatever you do will be correct. But if the true mind becomes overwhelmed by the false mind, and twisted and sullied, everything you do will be twisted and sullied. We speak of the true mind and the false mind, but it is not as if two things, black and white, existed side by side, separately. The true mind is what the mind is in its original state—something with which you are equipped since before your parents were born, but something which, because it is formless, neither comes into being nor ceases to exist. Your body has a form as given by your parents, but your formless mind cannot be said to have been given by your parents. The mind is what the body comes equipped with when a human being is born.

Zen and the Mind

Zen, I am told, is a school of religion intended to convey the true mind. I also hear that not all Zen men are the same because there is unauthentic Zen and many, while mouthing things that sound genuine, have not attained the true Way.

A false mind is a "temper," something that is personal. What is a temper? It is something that is caused by the blood. The blood moves and goes up, your face changes color, and anger shows. If someone hates what you love, you become angry and resentful, while if someone shares your sentiment and hates what you hate, you feel pleased and consider right what is wrong. If someone gives you what he treasures, you feel pleased as you accept it, you smile, and your face grows flushed with blood. Here again, you may consider right what is wrong. All this is because the temper in your body stirs up your flesh. The mind at such a time is called the false mind. When it rises, the true mind becomes eclipsed by it, and only bad things come to the fore.

Someone who has attained the Way deserves respect because he acts on the basis of his true mind, while diluting his false mind. Someone who has not attained the Way wins the reputation for being twisted and muddled because he allows his true mind to hide and his false mind to thrive, thereby doing nothing but things that do not confirm to the basic principle.

The *tanka* cited above has nothing "noble"[1] about it, but clearly manages to distinguish "evil" and "correct." A false mind is evil no matter what it does. If your false mind shows, you will lose in a sword fight, your arrow will not hit the mark, you will miss with your gun, you will not be able to ride a horse, your Nō dancing will look clumsy, your Nō chanting[2] will be unpleasant to listen to, and you will say wrong things when you open your mouth. Everything will go wrong.

If you follow the dictates of your true mind, however, everything should be all right. Suppose you set up something false and assert there is nothing false. Because such scheming comes from a false mind, its falsehood will be quickly revealed. If your mind is true, those who listen to you will know it in no time, without your explanation. A true mind does not require any explanation. A false mind is the disease of the mind. Ridding oneself of the false mind is ridding oneself of the disease. If you get rid of this disease, you will have a diseaseless mind. And the diseaseless mind is called the true mind. If you can meet the dictates of the true mind, you are a master of swordsmanship.

There is no field of endeavor to which this principle does not apply.

Mutō, *or No-Sword*[3]

"No-sword" does not necessarily mean that you are no good unless you can take your opponent's sword. Nor does it mean taking his sword and flaunting it to add to your honor. No-sword simply means having no sword—then you will try not to allow your opponent to slash you. Its true intent is never to make you say something like, "Now watch how I get his sword!"

---

[1] Take, *the original word for "noble," is a term often used in assessing a tanka.*

[2] *The original for "chanting" is* mai, *dancing.*

[3] *For all the importance of the concept of "no-sword," this "volume" is apparently counted as an extra.*

No-sword does not mean to try to take your opponent's sword at all cost when he tries to prevent you from taking it. No-sword also means not to try to take your opponent's sword when he tries to prevent you from doing so. Someone who is taken up by the thought of preventing his sword from being taken will forget to slash you, and while intent on not allowing you to get his sword, will not be able to slash you. Not being slashed is winning. No-sword is not meant to make a trick out of taking your opponent's sword. It is a skill you acquire of not allowing someone to slash you when you don't have a sword.

So-called no-sword is not a trick to take your opponent's sword, but is meant in order for you to use various instruments at will. If you can adopt as your sword even the one you have taken from your opponent when you do not have one, shouldn't you be able to make use of whatever else you may have on hand? Even with a fan you should be able to defeat an opponent equipped with a sword. No-sword means the readiness to do this. Suppose you are walking along with a bamboo stick, carrying no sword, when someone draws his long sword and assaults you. If you then parry with your stick, take away his sword (though you don't necessarily have to), and restrain him without being slashed, you win. Regard such a mind as what no-sword truly means.

No-sword means neither taking an opponent's sword nor slashing him. If your opponent is determined to slash you, take his sword. But taking the sword must not be your intent from the outset. It is intended for you to learn to make good estimates. You must learn to estimate how much distance is needed between your opponent and your body for his sword not to strike you. With a good estimate of this distance you need not fear the sword your opponent strikes out with, and when it does strike you, your mind will have enough flexibility left to measure the impact. You will not be able to take the opponent's sword as long as you stay far enough away not to be struck. You can take the sword only within the space in which it may touch you. Be slashed to take it.

No-sword is the readiness to allow your opponent a sword and fight him, with your own hands as your implements. The sword is long; the hands are short. It will be no good unless you get so close to your opponent as to be slashed at. You must calculate how your hands can fight the opponent's sword. This means you must devise some way of having the opponent's sword go past you so that you may put yourself under the hilt of the sword, move swiftly, and get hold of the sword. At the critical moment you must not tangle with your opponent. Even so, unless you get right next to him, you won't be able to wrest away the sword.[1]

No-sword is held to be the exclusive secret of this school. Postures, sword positions, the assessment of the fighting space, distance, movement, mental working, *tsuke,* assault, double-dealing—all these derive from the learning of no-sword. No-sword is central to all important things.

Daiki Taiyū[2]

Everything has a *tai,* noumenon, and a *yū,* phenomenon. Where there is a *tai,* there is a *yū.* For example, the bow is a *tai;* the acts of drawing it, shooting an arrow, and hitting the target are all *yū.* The lamp is a *tai;* the light is a *yū.* The water is a *tai;* the moisure is a *yū* of the water. The plum is a *tai;* when you speak of its fragrance or its coloration, you are speaking of its *yū.* The sword is a *tai;* slashing or thrusting is a *yū.*

In this sense, *ki,* mind, is a *tai,* and when things come out of the *ki* and work variously, they are called *yū.* Just as the flowers bloom, colors show, and a fragrance emanates because of the existence of the *tai* called plum, so do such moves as *tsuke, kake,* double-dealing, and *ken-tai* come outside because of the existence of the ready *ki* inside.[3] Such external workings are called *yū. Dai* of *daiki* means "great" and is honorific.

---

[1]*Muneyoshi notes that after working hard at the art of no-sword he reached a stage where, without a sword, he could defeat "six or seven out of ten [armed] men" or defeat one armed man "six or seven out of ten times."*

[2]*Ideograph by ideograph,* dai *of* daiki taiyū *is honorific;* ki, *mind;* tai, *noumenon, substance, thing-in-itself;* yū, *phenomenon, manifestation, application.* Daiki taiyū *is a Zen term, which as a phrase refers to the external manifestation of a mental movement, or simply freedom, the ability to do anything at will.*

[3]*Mitsuyoshi: "The readiness to regard any change on the opponent's part as coming from you is of primary importance. If your mind follows every changing indication on the part of your opponent, that means you are lagging. The thing to do is to force your opponent to follow your changes and, by following his resultant changes, to win."*

When a Zen monk comports himself freely and at will, and whatever he says, **101**
whatever he does, all meet the basic principle and echo logic, he is said to have
attained a divine ability, *daiki taiyū*. Divine ability or divine transformation does not
mean a mysterious doing of a demon or god descended from the void, but utter
freedom in doing anything. Numberless sword positions, double-dealing, traps, handling of various implements, leaping up, leaping back, grabbing a blade, kicking down,
moving variously, achieving freedom in other things than what you have learned[1]—all
this is called total *yū*. Unless you are internally equipped with a *ki* at all times, total *yū*
will not manifest itself.

Alertness

Even when you sit in someone's guest room, you first look up, then to the right and to
the left, and remain alert in case something falls on you from above without warning.
When you sit next to a sliding door, you must be alert in case it tumbles on you. When
you wait on a noble or a person of exalted rank, you must keep alert in case something
untoward occurs. Likewise, when you enter a gate or go out of one, you must not allow
yourself to be absentminded. To be thus constantly alert is possible with a *ki*.[2]

---

[1] *Reference to the Zen term* kyōge betsuden. *See* T'ai-a, *note, p. 125.*

[2] *These cautions were practical in an age when the swordsman had to be ever mindful of possible
entrapment or sudden assault from an assassin. In Kyoto there is still a noble's house that features a
guest room with a secret chamber tucked away adjacent to it; while the lord of the house was having
a guest, a couple of swordsmen hid themselves in the chamber, ready to leap out to protect their lord
or kill his guest.*

Some other pieces of advice that Munenori gives appear in Hoka no Mono no Koto *(Matters
Other Than Swordsmanship), a list of 119 admonitions he presented to Sakai, Governor of Sanuki,
in 1626:*

• *In someone's guest room you should note all the implements placed in it, whatever they may be.
Even in a guest room, choose a spot with a better view of everything. The points of your host's body
you should mark are the movements of his hands and arms. You should also pay attention to possible places through which to get out of the room. Try to put a distance of twelve feet between your
host and yourself.* (continued on page 102)

With a *ki* always inside, a swift, effective response may come when needed. Such a response is a *yū*. But if the *ki* is not ripe, no *yū* will show. If you maintain alertness in everything you do and accumulate experience, your *ki* will become ripe and *yū* will result. If your *ki* becomes stiff and rigid, there will be no *yū*. If your *ki* becomes ripe, it will extend throughout your body, and *yū* will show in your hands, feet, eyes, or in whichever part it may be needed.

In the face of someone with a great *ki* and *yū*, a swordsman who can do only what he has learned will not even be able to lift his finger. "Staring down" is not fiction. If someone with a great *ki* gives a stare, his opponent will be riveted to it and remain as he is, forgetting to draw his sword. If he lags by a blink, he is lost. When a cat stares, a rat will fall from the sky. Disconcerted by the cat's stare, the rat will make a misstep and drop. An unaccomplished fellow meeting a man with a great *ki* is like a rat meeting a cat.

* *Someone with a mind to deceive you tends to try to size you up even while handling various utensils, such as a tea spoon, or while serving cookies or tea. Do not take your mind from his arms. When both his hands are full, pay special attention to the moment they become free. When meeting two persons, pay attention to the one who has fewer things and talks less.*

* *At night, put the light far from you in your room. It is important that your sleeping position should not be visible.*

* *When you walk at night with a servant holding a lantern, have him light the road ahead while putting yourself in the dark. If someone comes, you may have your servant lift his lantern in the direction of the stranger.*

* *If you come across someone you are not sure of while walking on a road at night, quickly speak to him. Talk in such a way that the stranger may not really understand you as you stride up to him. While this is happening, you should be able to find out who he is. Someone with a nefarious intent is sure to be taken aback by this approach and lose heart.*

* *When you sleep in a mosquito net, put half of your sword outside it, tie the sword cord to the bottom hem of the net, and place the sword-securing loop attached to the swordguard inside the net. When something dangerous is expected, put your hand through this longer-than-usual loop before going to sleep.*

* *In your bedroom, never sleep right next to the sliding doors or screens. Put yourself away from them as far as their height.*

Great Yū

A Zen phrase says, "When a great *yū* manifests itself, it transcends rules."[1] A man of *daiki taiyū* does not at all concern himself either with things learned or with laws. In everything, there are things learned, laws, and proscriptions. Someone who has attained the ultimate state brushes them aside. He does things freely, at will. Someone who goes outside the laws and acts at will is called a man of *daiki taiyū*.

Ki is also a state where you remain watchful of things without any internal lapse. But if your watchfulness becomes excessive and turns rigid and stiff, you become bound by that watchfulness, and unfree. That is a *ki* not ripe yet. When you accumulate experience, your *ki* will become ripe, melt, and spread throughout your body. Then you can move freely. That state is called great *yū*.

Ki, the Door, and the Mind

Ki is also the "door of the mind" *(ki-*A*)*.[2] The term *ki* depends on where it is. The mind is the innermost quarter, and the *ki*-A is the entrance door. *Ki* is the door lock. Or think that the mind is the master of the body and therefore lives in its innermost quarter. The *ki*-A puts itself at the door and works outside for the master, the mind. The mind may be good or evil, depending on whether the *ki,* after leaving the door and going outside, does something good or something evil. The *ki*-A, when guarding the door and holding itself well, is the same as the *ki*.

Whether someone, after unlocking the door and going outside, does good or evil, or does something divinely spectacular, depends on the decision made before the door is unlocked. So the *ki* is of vital importance. If it works well, a great *yū* will show outside.

---

[1] *Soku 3*. Hekiganroku.

[2] *Homophones are used. The two words, both pronounced* ki, *are distinguished here as* ki *and* ki-A.

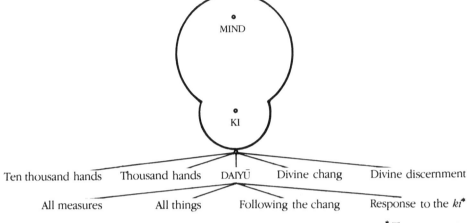

In short, you may not be wrong in thinking that the *ki* and the *ki*-A are the same thing. The distinction comes from where they are. Then again, even though I have spoken of "innermost quarters" and the "door," there are no set places in the body that may be so designated. These are all done in a manner of speaking. It is like someone's speech. You may say the beginning of a speech is the opening and the finishing part the ending. But in truth the spoken words themselves do not have any such fixable entities.

Shifting Mind

A verse by Manura the Holy One[1] says:

> *The mind shifts, following myriad scenes,*
> *how it shifts, barely perceived.*

[1]*Manura (died 825) is an Indian prince who became a prominent follower of Vasubandhu (ca. 420-500). A philosopher and writer, Vasubandhu, among other things, expounded the doctrine of "mind-only."*

This verse is held to be esoteric in Zen study. I quote it here because what it means is of vital importance to swordsmanship. Someone who does not study Zen may find it difficult to grasp at first.

"Myriad scenes" in swordsmanship would mean the countless moves your opponent makes. Your mind shifts at each of those moves. For example, if your opponent lifts his sword, your mind will shift to it; if he moves it to his right, your mind will shift to his right, and if he shifts it to his left, your mind will shift to his left. This is what the first line means.

What is crucial to swordsmanship is the second line, "how it shifts, barely perceived."[1] The mind does not leave its trace where it was, but is like "a boat that rows off, losing its trace in white waves,"[2] its trace vanishing as it moves forward, not stopping at all. "Barely perceived" means that your mind should not tarry here and there. If it tarries in one spot, you will lose the sword fight. If it stays rather than keeps shifting, that would be a disaster.

Because the mind has neither color nor shape, it is naturally invisible to the eye. But if it becomes "attached" and tarries, it is bound to become visible. It is like white cloth. It becomes scarlet if you transfer scarlet to it. It becomes purple if you transfer purple to it. The human mind too will reveal itself and become visible if transferred to something else. If you transfer your mind to boys and young men,[3] people will soon know. If you have some thought inside, it will show outwardly. If you intently watch your opponent's move and allow your mind to tarry there, you will be defeated.

The purpose of my quoting the verse above has been to say: Don't let your mind tarry. I will not bother to quote the remaining two lines. Learn the whole verse when you study Zen. For swordsmanship, the first two lines are adequate.

---

[1] *The ultimate sought by Munenori's school was* enten jizai, *or* marobashi —*the ability to shift the sword (and the mind) fluidly and at will.*

[2] *A* tanka *attributed to Sami Mansei, a poet of the eighth century. The version cited here appears as No. 1327 of the* Shūi Shū, *the third imperial anthology of Japanese poetry. In full it reads: "To what shall I compare this world? A boat that rows off at daybreak, losing its trace in white waves."*

[3] *Samurai frequently engaged in homosexual activities. The next sentence refers to a common theme in court poetry.*

106 *Swordsmanship and Buddhism*

Swordsmanship agrees with Buddhism and is in accord with Zen in many ways. It abhors attachment, the state of tarrying with something. This is the crucial point. Not tarrying is of vital importance. Consider the *tanka* the prostitute of Eguchi wrote in response to Priest Saigyō:[1]

> *I hear you're someone who's left his home;*
> *Don't let your mind tarry, I only wish, in this temporary hut*

For swordsmanship there should be nothing wrong in giving deep thought to the second half of this tanka. No matter what secretly transmitted technique you may use, if you allow your mind to tarry on it, you will lose your fight. Be it your opponent's move or your own, in slashing or in thrusting, the important thing is to train your mind so that it may not tarry in anything.

Lung-chi's Words

Lung-chi[2] once told his congregation:

[1] *Reference to the famous exchange of* tanka *between the priest-poet Saigyō (1118-1190) and a prostitute who worked at the river port of Eguchi in present-day Osaka. One day, after he had paid his respects at a temple, Saigyō ran into a rainstorm and asked for lodging at a nearby brothel. When the prostitute who came out declined his request, Saigyō composed a* tanka *which went: "Difficult though things may be until discarding this world, you even refuse me temporary lodging." "Discarding this world" means taking Buddhist vows. "Temporary lodging" is a metaphor for this life, as opposed to the afterlife. In the prostitute's response, "leaving one's home" also means taking Buddhist vows, and the "temporary hut," this life. The exchange provides the basis for the Nō drama* Eguchi, *attributed to Kan'ami (1333-1384). A popular belief held that the prostitute was in fact an incarnation of Samanthadhabra, the deity of compassion.*

[2] *A Chinese Zen master (1529-1588).*

Don't see a pillar in this pillar that exists,
don't see a pillar in this pillar that does not.
Completely discard existence and nonexistence,
and grasp the truth behind the two.

We are told to apply these words to everything we do. I quote them here because, as a certain man of wisdom[1] indicated, they have a connection with swordsmanship.

The pillar that exists and the pillar that does not mean existence and nonexistence, good and evil, which are sure to exist in our mind, rising like pillars. To keep in our mind the pillar that exists is bad enough; to keep the pillar that does not is even worse. So the advice is: Don't see either pillar. Existence and nonexistence, good and evil, are all diseases of the mind. Unless you rid your mind of these diseases, it will not be any good no matter what you do. Hence: "Completely discard existence and non-existence, / and grasp the truth behind the two." Discard existence and nonexistence. Live instead in the middle of both. Advance and rise to the ultimate state while within the two. Even when you have attained the Buddhist Law, you will be truly grateful to the discerning eye that transcends existence and nonexistence.

Discard Even the True Law

"Discard even the True Law, let alone the false ones."[2]

Once you have understood something, don't let it stay in your mind, even if it is the True Law. Even the True Law will be dust once you have understood it. Nothing need be said of false laws. After seeing all the principles, do not let any of them stay in your mind. Slash them away, one after another, and keep your mind empty so that you may conduct yourself with a natural mind.

[1] *Takuan.*
[2] *Source unidentified. "The True Law" is Buddhist Law.*

108   Unless you attain that state, you can hardly be called a master of swordsmanship. I here speak of swordsmanship because that is our family concern. But this observation is not limited to swordsmanship, it is applicable to every other field of endeavor. If you are conscious of swordsmanship while employing it, that is a disease. If you are conscious of shooting an arrow while doing so, you are diseased with archery. If you make your mind natural in employing a sword or a bow, you should be free with the sword, have no difficulty with the bow. A natural mind that nothing can take by surprise is good in everything. If you lose your mind in a normal state and try to say something you feel you must say at any cost, your voice will tremble. If you lose your natural mind in writing in the presence of other people, your hand will tremble. A natural mind is one that has nothing left in it; everything is slashed away, and it is empty. Readers of Confucian books do not comprehend this principle of empty mind, but concern themselves exclusively with the meaning of the ideograph *kei*.[1] A mind concerned with the ideograph *kei* is not in the ultimate state. I am told it is only in the first or second stage of training.

The second and third volumes are entitled "Death-Dealing Blade" and "Life-Giving Sword." A blade that kills people is in truth a sword that allows them to live. In a disturbed world, many people are killed without cause. A death-dealing blade is used to bring peace to such a world; but once peace is achieved, the same blade becomes a life-giving sword, does it not?

[1] *See pp. 77.*

The first volume of this book of swordsmanship, called The Shoe-Offering Bridge,
is largely a catalogue. It has been handed down directly from my late father the
Governor of Tajima, Muneyoshi and Kamiizumi, the Governor of Musashi, Fujiwara-
Hidetsuna. This catalogue is to be copied and given to anyone who has mastered the
art, as proof of its transmittal.

The other two volumes contain thoughts developed after what was initially
learned.[1] My father pondered this art all his life, not forgetting it even while sleeping or
eating. As a result, he learned some subtle principles and, with me near him, he would
talk daily about the subtleties and explain the profundities. Whenever there was any-
thing I thought I understood at all, I would sincerely tuck it away in my mind.[2] As an
adult, I took up the sword and inherited my father's profession, though I have yet to
master freedom. But when I passed "the age of knowing my destiny,"[3] I began to have a
taste for this art. Since then, every time I've learned a principle, I've recorded it. The
accumulation here covers a number of things. Ultimately, however, everything returns
to the "one mind"; the "one mind" extends to many things, which in turn converge in
the "one mind." This is the point.

Now that I have written these two volumes, I will bequeath them, along with the
first volume, to my house.[4]

Ninth Month in the Ninth Year of Kan'ei (1632)

Kamiizumi, Governor of Musashi,

        Fujiwara Hidetsuna

The Late Father Yagyū, Governor of Tajima,

        Taira Muneyoshi

His Son Yagyū, Governor of Tajima,

        Taira Munenori

---

[1] *"What was initially learned" refers to the fighting patterns and other teachings developed by the*
founder of the Shinkage School, Kamiizumi Hidetsuna.

[2] *"Sincerely tuck it away," etc., is a phrase that appears in Book 8,* The Doctrine of the Mean, *where*
Confucius praises his beloved student, Yen Yūan.

[3] *Fifty years of age.*

[4] *The entire passage is written in Chinese.*

Fudōchi Shinmyō Roku

Divine Record of Immovable Wisdom

The Mind That Tarries

Suppose you see in a glance a sword coming at you and decide to block it with your own. Then your mind stays with the sword and, neglecting your own moves, you allow the opponent to slash you. This is called the mind that tarries.

Suppose you do see the opponent's sword come, but do not allow your mind to stay with it. Suppose, instead, that in response to the coming sword, you do not think of striking back or form any idea or judgment, but the moment you see the sword raised you move in, your mind not tarrying, and grasp the sword. Then you should be able to wrest from the opponent the sword intended to slash you, and turn it into one with which to slash him....

In Buddhism, the mind that tarries is called *māyā.*[1]

---

[1] *Illusion, ignorance.*

Fudōchi, *or Immovable Wisdom*

Fudō [in the term *fudōchi*] does not mean the immobility of a stone or a tree. The mind which moves over there, to the left, to the right, in the ten directions and in the eight directions, but does not tarry anywhere for a second, has *fudōchi*....

Likewise, the Fudō Myō-ō[1] symbolizes the human mind that does not move, the body that does not unsettle. Not unsettling means not staying with anything.

Glancing at something and not allowing the mind to stay with it is called *fudō*. If your mind stays with something, the various judgments that are in your head will begin to stir variously. The mind that stays is not moving even if it appears to be.

For example, suppose ten men come at you, each with a sword. If you deal with each one and do not allow your mind to stay with what you do, forgetting one move in order to deal with the next, you should be able to let yourself work adequately with all ten of them.

Going Back to the Starting Point

Now, when someone who has trained from the beginner's stage reaches the rank of "immovable wisdom," he is said to turn around and settle back to where he began. To explain this in relation to your swordsmanship, the beginner does not even know how to hold his sword, so there is no way for his mind to tarry. If someone strikes at him, he instinctively responds, giving no particular thought to it.

As he learns various things, however, and as you teach him how to hold up his sword, where to put his mind, and many other things, his mind comes to tarry in many places, and even when striking at someone he comes to feel not entirely free in many ways. But days, months, and years pile up, and as he continues to train, he becomes oblivious of his mind, whatever posture he may take or however he may hold his sword. In the end he comes to feel as he did at the outset, when he knew nothing, had learned nothing.

[1] *The Fudō Myō-ō (Immovable Bright King) is a Japanese name for Acala, an angry manifestation of Vairocana, the central Sun. As Takuan explains, this deity "grips a sword in his right hand and holds a rope in his left, with teeth bared, eyes furious." In Japan he is usually depicted as seated on a rock, enveloped in giant flames.*

Scarecrow as the Ultimate Case   *113*

The National Teacher Bukkoku of Kamakura[1] has this poem:

> *Though he doesn't have the mind to stand guard,*
>   *not useless in the mountain paddy is that scarecrow*

This applies to everything.

A scarecrow in a mountain paddy is a doll equipped with a bow and an arrow. Birds and beasts see it and run away. The doll has no mind whatsoever, but because deer become frightened and run away and its purpose is met, it is not all useless. What it does is comparable to the deed of someone who has reached the ultimate stage in any field of endeavor. In such a person, only the arms and legs and the body work, and as the mind does not tarry anywhere for a second, you cannot tell where it is. Without thought, without mind, he thus attains the rank of the scarecrow.

An ordinary mortal who is completely stupid cannot make himself conspicuous, because he has no wisdom in the first place. Similarly, an outstanding man of wisdom does not make himself conspicuous because he has reached the depths. It is the knowing fellow whose wisdom shows who is funny. You must find the behavior of monks these days funny. I am embarrassed by it.

Noumenon and Phenomenon

We speak of noumenal training and phenomenal training.

Noumenal training, as I said earlier, aims for the state where you do not concern yourself with anything and you discard your mind. Its stages are as I have written above.

Without phenomenal training, however, all you will have will be theories in your head, and neither your arms nor your legs will work. Phenomenal training, as applied to swordsmanship, entails the "five points"[2] concerning posture and the various other things to be learned.

---

[1] *A Japanese Zen monk (1241-1316).*
[2] *See p. 24.*

Even if you knew the noumenon, it would be useless unless you could employ techniques freely. Similarly, even if you could handle your sword well, it would not be any good if you were in the dark about the state where the noumenon ultimately lies. Noumenon and phenomenon ought to be like the two wheels of a cart.

Without Enough Space of Time

There is a phrase, "without enough space of time to allow a strand of hair...." For example, when you clap your hands, the sound comes out instantaneously. Between the clapping and the sound is there not enough space to allow a strand of hair. It is not as if you clap your hands, then the sound thinks about it and comes out after a space of time. The same moment you clap your hands, the sound comes out.

If your mind stays with the sword that someone swings at you, a space of time will result. During that space of time your own move will be forgotten. If even a strand of hair can't get in between the moment your opponent strikes at you and the moment you react, the opponent's sword might as well be yours.

Zen dialogue stresses this responsive mind. Buddhism abhors the mind that stops and stays with something, and calls it *kleśa.*[1] What is prized is the mind that flows torrentially and never stops, like a ball riding a swift current.

Zen Sect

In the Zen sect, if asked, "What on earth is the Buddha?" you are to raise your fist.[2] If asked, "What is the ultimate meaning of Buddhist Law?" you are to say, even before the

[1] *Trouble, anxiety, illusion.*

[2] *Allusion to a passage in* The Great Collection of Zen Koan: *"The Zen monk Pieh-feng-yin on one occasion asked Yüan-wu, 'What did sages of old use to hold in meeting someone?' The master at once firmly raised his fist." Also, Soku 11,* Mumonkan, *which is based on* Chao-chou's Words: *"Chao-chou on one occasion went to the place of a hermit and asked, 'Are you there? Are you there?' The hermit at once firmly raised his fist." Yüan-wu (1063-1135) is a Chinese Zen master whose commentaries form an important part of the* Hekiganroku. *Chao-chou (778-897), another Chinese Zen master, figures prominently in both the* Mumonkan *and the* Hekiganroku.

question is finished, "A spray of plum flowers,"[1] or "An oak tree in the garden."[2] The point is to not deliberate on the right or wrong of your response. What is prized is the mind that does not stay.

Knowing the Mind

To explain the mind with words, it exists in others as well as in yourself, and does good or evil things day and night, in accordance with its karma. The mind leaves the house or destroys a country, and depending on its owner, it may be good or evil. Because, however, few explore and bring to light what the mind is really like, everyone continues to be misled by the mind....Those who happen to have brought its nature to light have a hard time putting what has been learned into practice.

The ability to speak eloquently of the mind may not mean enlightenment on the subject. Even if you hold forth on water, your mouth does not become wet. Even if you speak eloquently of fire, your mouth does not become hot. You cannot know the real water and real fire without touching them; you cannot know them just by explaining them from books. Likewise, even if you speak eloquently of food, hunger will not be cured. The ability to speak is not enough for knowing the subject at hand.

In our society, both Buddhists and Confucians expound on the mind. But as long as they do not behave as they preach, they have yet to know the mind. Until each person explores the mind in himself and knows it fully, the matter will remain unclear.

Place for the Mind

Where to put your mind?

If you put your mind in the move of the opponent's body, you will be distracted by that move. If you put it in his sword, you will be distracted by his sword. If you put it in your desire to strike the opponent, you will be distracted by that desire. If you put it

[1]Allusion to a line of verse, "A spray of plum flowers is in harmony with snow and fragrant," in Zenrin Kushū (A Zen Phrase Anthology), compiled in 1574.
[2]Soku 37, Mumonkan. One of the most famous Zen exchanges.

in your own sword, you will be distracted by your sword. If you put it in your desire not to be struck, you will be distracted by that desire. If you put it in the opponent's posture, you will be distracted by his posture. In short, there is no place to put your mind, they say.

Someone said: "If you put your mind elsewhere, it will stay in whatever place it has gone to, and you will be defeated by your opponent. So stuff your mind into the area under your navel[1] and don't let it go anywhere. Simply keep it rolling in response to the opponent's moves."

This is understandable. Nonetheless, from the viewpoint of an advanced stage in Buddhism, to stuff the mind under the navel to prevent it from going elsewhere is low, not advanced, in stage.... [In any event,] if you stuff your mind under your navel in your attempt not to let it go elsewhere, you will be distracted by that attempt and end up not taking full initiatives, not feeling very free.

Someone asked: "If stuffing my mind under my navel hampers my moves, makes me feel unfree, and prevents me from taking full initiatives, where in my body shall I put it?"

I responded by saying: "If you put it in your right hand, you will be distracted by your right hand and won't be able to take full initiatives. If you put it in your eyes, you will be distracted by them and won't be able to take full initiatives. If you put it in your right foot, you will be distracted by your right foot and won't be able to take full initiatives. No matter where it may be, if you put your mind in one place, any of the other places won't be able to take full initiatives."

"Well, then, where shall I put it?"

"If you don't put it anywhere," I said, "your mind will fill your whole body, extend and spread all over. Then, it will serve your hand when the hand needs it, your foot when the foot needs it, your eyes when the eyes need it. Because it fully exists wherever it is needed, it will serve any place it is needed....

"If you stop thinking of some place to put it, your mind is bound to extend and spread all over and fill your whole body. Without putting your mind in any place, you must let it serve wherever it is needed at each moment, depending on your opponent's move....

---

[1] *The area of the stomach under the navel is thought to be a place where courage and health are generated.*

"Devising ways not to let your mind stay in one place depends entirely on training. Not letting your mind stay anywhere is the goal and of vital importance. If you don't put it anywhere, it will be everywhere."[1]

The Be-Mind and the No-Mind

The be-mind *(ushin)* is the same as the "false mind" *(mō-shin)*. It is the "mind that exists," and becomes one-sided about anything. We call such a mind the be-mind because it has things to think about and thereby generates ideas and judgments. The no-mind *(mushin)* is the same as the "true mind" *(honshin)*. Neither congealing nor taking definite shape, it is a mind devoid of ideas and judgments, a mind that extends and spreads throughout your body, filling your whole being....

If the no-mind becomes a good part of you, you will not stay with one thing or neglect a single thing. It will be in your body like brimming water, coming out and serving whenever needed....

If you have something to think about in your mind, you are but are not hearing someone speaking to you. This is because your mind stays with that something you are thinking about. Your mind tilts to one side with that something, and as it does, you don't hear while hearing, you don't see while seeing....

If you try to rid your mind of that something, that attempt, in turn, becomes something in your mind. If you don't try, that something will go away on its own, leaving you with the no-mind.

[1] *On the same point, Miyamoto Musashi has this to say in* A Book of Five Rings: *"In the way of swordsmanship, hold your mind in a manner no different from your normal mind. Let it be not at all different in normal life or in a sword fight, not pulling it too hard, not allowing it to become slack in any way. Place it at the center of your being, lest it become lopsided. Let it remain fluid, and even at the very moment of letting it become fluid, try preventing it from ceasing to be fluid."*

An Empty Gourd on the Water

If you put an empty gourd on the water and touch it, it will slip to one side. No matter how you try, it won't stay in one spot. The mind of someone who has reached the ultimate state does not stay with anything, even for a second. It is like an empty gourd on the water that is pushed around.

Throw Your Mind Away

Don't let your mind stay with hands that are holding a sword about to strike. Forget your striking hands. Simply strike and slash your opponent. Don't put your mind in your opponent. Keep in mind that the opponent is void, you are void, and so are your striking sword and your hands holding it. And never be distracted by the voidness of it all.

The Zen master Wu-hsüeh of Kamakura,[1] when captured and about to be beheaded during the War of Great T'ang,[2] said in verse: "Like a flash of lightning cut the spring breeze!"[3] At this, we are told, the man about to behead him threw down his sword and ran away.

Wu-hsüeh must have meant this: The moment the sword is swung up is like a flash of lightning, with no mind or idea in it. There is no mind in the striking sword, in the executioner, or in me, the man being executed. The executioner is void, the sword is void, and so am I, the man about to be struck. The man striking is not a man, his

[1] *Wu-hsüeh, also known as the National Teacher Bukkō (1226-1286): A Buddhist of the Southern Sung. He went to Japan at the invitation of the shogun Hōjō Tokimune (1251-1284), who repelled two attempts by Kublai Khan (1216-1296) to invade Japan. Wu-hsüeh became the founder of the Engaku temple of Kamakura and greatly influenced the Ji sect of Buddhism.*

[2] *Reference to the Southern Sung's last major attempt, in 1275, to resist Kublai Khan's conquest of China.*

[3] *The entire verse, a quatrain, may be translated: "With no space for erecting a single staff in the whole universe, / I'm pleased to see that man, void, and law are all void. / I prize the three-foot sword of Great Yüan, / which like a flash of lightning cuts the spring breeze!" Yüan is the dynasty Kublai Khan established in China.*

THE SWORD AND THE MIND

striking sword is not a sword, and I, about to be struck, am no more than a flash of lightning. So cutting me is like cutting a wind blowing in the spring sky. Nothing stays, that's it. Soldier, cutting a wind, you won't feel a thing.

When you do everything like this, completely forgetting your mind, you have attained the rank of a superior hand. When you dance a dance, you take up a fan and take steps. When you do so, as long as you can't forget yourself, trying to improve the movements of your hands and feet and to dance a dance better, you can't say you are accomplished. While your mind stays with your hands and feet, your performance won't be interesting. Whatever you do while you haven't discarded your mind altogether will be bad.

Seek the Released Mind

This is Mencius' word.[1] What it means is that you must search and seek the mind that has been released and bring it back to yourself. For example, if your dog, cat, or chicken is released and goes off some place, you will search and seek it and bring it home. Similarly, if your mind, which is your master, takes to an evil path and runs away, why don't you seek it and bring it home, says Mencius.[2] This is quite understandable.

Nevertheless, a man by the name of Shao K'ang Chieh[3] said, "You must release your mind." This is just the reverse. What he means is that if you keep your mind in check, it will become exhausted and won't work like a cat, and that therefore lest your mind stay with you and become tainted, you must use it well, leave it alone, and chase it off, wherever it may be.

The mind becomes tainted and stays on, so don't let it get tainted, don't let it stay on, but find it and bring it back to yourself—this is what you say to someone at the beginner's stage. Try to become like a lotus that does not become tainted with mud.

[1] *Mencius (371-289? B.C.): Chinese philosopher.*

[2] *Book IX, Part 1,* The Book of Mencius.

[3] *Shao K'ang Chieh (1011-1077): Chinese philosopher who argued that the universe is no more than a manifestation of one's mind. One of those delightful eccentrics who dot Chinese history, Shao is said to have lived happily among the poor and to have refused to work for the government despite repeated invitations.*

120   There's nothing wrong with being in the mud. A well-polished ball of crystal does not become tainted even in the mud. Treat the mind like a ball of crystal, and let it go where it wants to.

If you constrain your mind, you will be unfree. You put your mind on a tight rein only while you are a beginner. If you continue to do so all your life, you will never reach the advanced stage, but end up remaining at a low stage.

While you are in training, the state of mind that Mencius prescribes, "Seek the released mind," will work well. At the ultimate stage, what you need is Shao K'ang Chieh's dictum, "You must release your mind."

Taia Ki

On the T'ai-a[1]

It may be said that the swordsman neither vies in a contest, nor concerns himself with strength or weakness, nor advances or retreats a single step. His opponent does not see him; he does not see his opponent.[2] If he concentrates on the area where heaven and earth remain unseparated and yin and yang do not show, he should achieve success straightforwardly.

The accomplished man does not kill people by using his sword; he lets them live by using his sword. When he wants to kill them, he does so instantaneously; when he wants to let them live, he does so instantaneously. He can kill or give life at will. Without seeing good and bad, he makes the distinction well; without making a judgment, he judges well. He can walk on the water as if on the ground; he can walk on the ground as if on the water. Someone with that freedom can in no way be affected by anyone on earth. He is simply one of a kind.

[1]*Any of the three mythical swords wrought by Fēng Hu-tzu in ancient China.*

[2]*The opponent is unable to see the swordsman's noumenon; the swordsman, on the other hand, is able to see beyond his opponent's noumenon, so the opponent's existence ceases to matter.*

If you wish to achieve that state, you must never neglect to think resourcefully. Whether walking, standing, sitting, or lying, whether talking or being silent, or whether sipping tea or having a meal, you must be prepared for an emergency, explore each matter to the full, and after having done so, penetrate into the matter. After countless months and numberless years, you will attain the desired state as naturally as you see a lamp in the darkness. Then you will acquire the wisdom that is not taught by your master[1] and generate exquisite usefulness that is not intended.[2] Precisely at that stage you will find yourself not just out of the ordinary, but far and away from the ordinary. Then you will be equal to the T'ai-a.

This magic sword of T'ai-a is held by everyone and is to be refined by each person. Someone who is enlightened by this will be feared by the Demon of Heaven; someone who is in the dark about it will be deceived by a heretic.

When two accomplished hands exchange sharp blows and neither wins, it is like the time when the Lord Buddha showed a lotus flower and Mahākāśyapa smiled,[3] or like knowing three things upon seeing one. The ability to tell the smallest difference in weight at one glance is common to such intuitive minds.[4] If it were someone who has completely resolved the ultimate question, he would instantaneously cut up anyone into three pieces before one is shown and three are understood. Would it be necessary for him to meet anyone face to face?

[1] *"Wisdom that is not taught by your master" is wisdom one acquires after being enlightened by ultimate truth.*

[2] *Something done intentionally is impure and unnatural.*

[3] *Mahākāśyapa was one of the Buddha's ten greatest disciples. When the Buddha, before his death, showed a lotus flower to the eighty thousand people gathered around him, Mahākāśyapa responded with a smile. The Buddha then saw that only Mahākāśyapa understood the Law.*

[4] *Soku 1*, Hekiganroku.

Such a person would not even flash the tip of his sword, being swifter than lightning, faster than a sudden storm. Someone without that skill, whose mind is likely to become attached or stuck to something, ends up breaking his own sword or cutting his own hand, and cannot be called a good swordsman. True swordsmanship cannot be conveyed through words; it cannot be learned through gestures. If there is a principle to be conveyed by means other than teaching,[1] this is it.

When ultimate freedom manifests itself, rules cease to exist.[2] "Obeying or disobeying the Way becomes unfathomable even to heaven."[3] How can that be possible? Someone of old said, "I have no picture of the *Pai-tse* in my house, because there is no such monster."[4] Someone who trains hard and attains that state of mind will be able to pacify the world with a single sword. May no one who studies swordsmanship be frivolous!

[1]*Kyōge betsuden, here translated "conveyed by means other than teaching," is a way of attaining enlightenment particularly stressed in Zen. As an independent phrase, it may loosely be translated as "the truth conveyed by means other than the doctrinal teachings."*

[2]*Soku 3, Hekiganroku.*

[3]*A line from a Buddhist verse by Eika Genkaku.*

[4]*The* Pai-tse *is an imaginary creature of China with the body of a bull and the head of a human. In the belief that it ate nightmares and troubles, a picture of the animal used to be hung in the house. The meaning of the statement appears to be that if you achieve a transcendental state of mind, you can avoid all troubles.*

126

Brief Annotated Bibliography

IN JAPANESE

Yagyū Family

Imamura, Yoshio. *Shiryō Yagyū Shinkage-ryū.* Tokyo: Shin Jinbutsu Ōrai Sha, 1967. 2 vols. An invaluable compilation of Yagyū documents, plus a history and commentary. Unfortunately the texts are not annotated and the two volumes are out of print.

———*Yagyū Ichizoku.* Tokyo: Shin Jinbutsu Ōrai Sha, 1971. An authentic examination of prominent Yagyū swordsmen and people who became their friends. Scholarly, well written.

Yagyū, Mitsuyoshi. *Tsuki no Sho.* Ed. Imamura Yoshio. Niigata: Nojima Shuppan, 1971. The most important treatise on swordsmanship by Munenori's son. The annotation is minimal.

Yagyū, Munenori. "Heihō Kaden Sho." *Kinsei Geidō Ron.* Ed. Nishiyama Matsunosuke and others. Tokyo: Iwanami Shoten, 1972. Pp. 301-343. Annotated by Watanabe Ichirō, this is the only text of its kind I know.

Yagyū, Muneyoshi. "Shinkage-ryū Heihō Mokuroku," *Kinsei Geidō Ron.* Pp. 345-354. The photographic reproductions of the fighting postures that are part of the present book were prepared from this text.

128   *Takuan*

Haga, Kōshirō. *Takuan.* Kyoto: Tankō Sha, 1979. A catalogue of Takuan's calligraphy and draw-
ings, with a biography. Scholarly, concise.

Ichikawa, Hakugen. *Takuan.* Tokyo: Kōdan Sha, 1978. Translations into modern Japanese of the
Fudōchi Shinmyō Roku and five other writings by Takuan, with the original texts, plus a
biography and philosophical commentary. The author's critical remarks on Zen, though
mild, are valuable.

Ikeda, Satoshi. *Fudōchi Shinmyō Roku.* Tokyo: Tokuma Shoten, 1970. Translations into modern
Japanese of the *Fudōchi Shinmyō Roku* and two other writings by Takuan with the original
texts. The author is somewhat parochial, but the book is readily available and easy to read.

IN ENGLISH

Chang, Wing-tsit, ed. and comp. *A Source Book in Chinese Philosophy.* Princeton, N.J.: Princeton
University Press, 1963. A large compilation of Chinese philosophical tracts from the beginnings to the modern times.

Chuang Tzu. *The Complete Works of Chuang Tzu.* Trans. Burton Watson. New York and London:
Columbia University Press, 1968. A best-selling translation of an important Taoist book.

Clausewitz, Carl von. *On War.* Ed. Anatol Rapoport. Middlesex, Eng.: Penguin Books, 1968. Often
cited in comparison with Sun Tsu's *Art of War,* for which see below.

Creel, G. Herrlee. *What Is Taoism? And Other Studies in Chinese Cultural History.* Chicago:
University of Chicago Press, 1970. The lead article clarifies the various concepts of *tao,*
"The Way."

Hoffman, Yoel, trans. with commentary. *The Sound of the One Hand: 281 Zen Koans with
Answers.* New York: Basic Books, 1975. Exactly what the title says.

Humphreys, Christmas. *A Popular Dictionary of Buddhism.* New York: The Citadel Press, 1963.
The book is convenient, and I hope it is still available.

Japan Society. *Nippon-tō: Art Swords of Japan.* The catalogue of a Japan Society exhibition in
1976. A detailed and beautifully printed introduction to the Japanese sword.

Katō, Bunnō, and others, eds., and Soothill, W.E., and others, rev. *The Threefold Lotus Sutra.* New
York and Tokyo: John Weatherhill, 1975. This contains three basic Buddhist *sutras.*

Kern, H., trans. *Saddharma-Pundarika or the Lotus of the True Law.* New York: Dover Publications, 1963. A classic translation of the most important Buddhist *sutra.*

Luk, Charles, trans. and ed. *The Vimalakirti Nirdesa Sutra.* Berkeley and London: Shambhala,
1972. One of the more important texts of Zen Buddhism.

Miyamoto, Musashi. *A Book of Five Rings.* Trans. Victor Harris. New York: The Overlook Press,
1974. A famous book on swordsmanship by Munenori's contemporary.

Morris, Ivan. *The Nobility of Failure: Tragic Heroes in the History of Japan.* New York: Holt, Rinehart and Winston, 1975. Scholarly, well written, and incisive. One of the tragic heroes described is Amakusa Shirō (1622-1638), the sixteen-year-old leader of the Shimabara rebellion, in which Munenori was indirectly involved.

Nitobe, Inazo. *Bushido: The Warrior's Code.* Burbank Calif.: Ohara Publications, 1975. Originally published in 1899, this presents an idealized view of *bushidō.*

Ōmori, Sōgen. "Zen Sword: Comments on the Fudōchi-shimmyōroku of Zen Master Takuan." *Chanoyu Quarterly,* No. 30, pp. 53-67. A good introduction to Takuan's famous treatise.

Rice, Edward. *Eastern Definitions.* Garden City, N.Y.: Doubleday, 1978. A new dictionary of Eastern religions.

Richie, Donald. *Zen Inklings.* New York and Tokyo: John Weatherhill, 1982. A collection of Zen stories by an authority on Japan's popular culture.

Sekida, Katsuki, trans. with commentary. *Two Zen Classics: Mumonkan & Hekiganroku.* New York and Tokyo: John Weatherhill, 1977. A full translation of the *Mumonkan* and a partial translation of the *Hekiganroku.*

Shaw, R.D.M., trans. and ed., with commentary. *The Blue Cliff Records: The Hekigan Roku.* London: Michael Joseph, 1961. The commentaries are fuller than those in *Two Zen Classics.*

Shibayama, Zenkei. *Zen Comments on the Mumonkan.* Trans. Sumiko Kudo. New York: New American Library, 1974. A complete translation of the *Mumonkan,* with a full commentary.

Sun Tzu. *The Art of War.* Tr. and with an introduction by Samuel B. Griffith. Oxford: Oxford Univ. Press, 1963. A famous Chinese tract on the art of waging war, translated and analyzed by a sinologue and brigadier general, U.S. Marine Corps. The translation incorporates comments by several prominent Chinese scholars, and the appendices include a complete translation of the tract on the same subject by Wu Tzu, who is often mentioned with Sun Tzu. A more recent edition by the popular author James Clavell (New York: Delacorte Press, 1983) is Lionel Giles' translation, pub. 1910, with which Clavell took "a few liberties." The text incorporates Giles' comments.

Suzuki, Daisetz T. *Zen and Japanese Culture.* Princeton, N.J.: Princeton Univ. Press, 1959. One of the most influential books on Zen and Japanese culture, this book, upon closer examination, may have some silly spots. It gives generous space to the ideas of Yagyū Munenori and Takuan and translates excerts from their writings.

Turnbull, S.R. *The Samurai: A Military History.* New York: Macmillan, 1977. A thorough history of Japanese fighting men and their battles from the beginnings to the second half of the nineteenth century.

Waley, Arthur. *Three Ways of Thought in Ancient China.* Garden City, N.Y.: Doubleday, 1956 (?). Originally published in 1939, this book examines Chuang Tzu, Mencius, and the Realists.

130

————*The Way and Its Power: A Study of the Tao Te Ching and Its Place in Chinese Thought.* New York: Grove Press, 1958. This should be read along with Creel's book, cited earlier.

Warner, Gordon, and Donn F. Draeger. *Japanese Swordsmanship: Technique and Practice.* New York and Tokyo: John Weatherhill, 1982. Mainly about *iai-dō* and its history. More practical than theoretical.

Yamamoto, Tsunetomo. *Hagakure.* Trans. William Scott Wilson. Tokyo, New York, and San Francisco: Kodansha International, 1979. Excerpts from a famous tract on samurai behavior that contains the dictum: "The way of the warrior, I've decided, is to die."

Glossary

bōshin [concentrated mind]: The spot where the [opponent's] mind is concentrated or reveals itself; namely, the part of the [opponent's] body where his next move is likely to be revealed first.

daiki taiyū: A Zen term meaning "utter freedom." See also *tai* and *yū*.

disease: The mind preoccupied in one way or another, be it for a second or for a considerable span of time.

double-dealing [*hyōri*]: A form of stratagem. The word, which in the original also means "double-talk" or "deception," is used in a positive sense by Munenori.

enten jizai [smoothly turning and being at will]: The ability to shift the sword and the mind at will. Same as *marobashi*, which see.

fudōchi [immovable wisdom]: The mind that has become so resilient as not to be "moved" by anything—or not to become stuck or attached to any noumenon or phenomenon. This seemingly contradictory notion appears to be based on the philosophical speculation that the state of ultimate movement is the same as that of nonmovement.

fukuro-shinai: A sword made of bamboo and leather.

heihō: A term that may mean any of the following: swordsmanship, sword fight, stratagem, strategy, tactics, the art of war.

Hekiganroku [Blue Cliff Record]:   A Chinese Zen classic, which is based on 100 koans collected by the Zen monk and poet Hsüeh-t'ou (980-1052) and the comments on them by the Zen monk Yüan-wu (1062-1135). The text as we know it seems to date from around 1300.

inka: A Buddhist certificate for maturity in training; later adopted in the martial arts.

jo-ha-kyū [introduction, development, finale]:   Originally, dance music terms. In Yagyū swordsmanship, the terms are used to describe three separate fighting techniques, three stages in a single move, as well as three states of mind.

kake: A form of attack.

kan: Insight.

kei [in Chinese, *ching*; respect, reverence]:   An important concept for Confucians, regarded as especially important by the Confucian scholars of the Sung dynasty (960-1234).

ken: (1) Assault; attack stance; or the state of mind in that stance; (2) sword; (3) observation.

ken-tai: Attack and waiting stances.

kenzen itchi [unity of swordsmanship and Zen]:   The state where the mastery of the mind achieved through swordsmanship is equal to that achieved in Zen training.

ki: (1) Mind; spirit; (2) chance.

kishōmon: A written pledge to train as a student. See also *seishi.*

kleśa: A Buddhist term meaning trouble, anxiety, or illusion.

koku: A measuring unit. When used in measuring rice, one *koku* represents about five bushels, an amount that was thought to be adequate to sustain an adult for a year during the Tokugawa period (1603-1868) and before. As a unit for measuring rice, it was also used to indicate the holdings or income of the samurai class.

kyōge betsuden: Conveying or attaining enlightenment or truth by means other than doctrinal teachings; or enlightenment or truth so conveyed or attained.

marobashi [letting (something) roll]:   The ability to shift the sword and the mind at will. Same as *enten jizai,* which see.

michi: In a spiritual context, the meaning of the word is akin to "the Way"; in other contexts, it may mean "field," as in the field of literature, and "art," as in the art of paper making.

Mumonkan [Gateless Gate]:   A Chinese Zen classic compiled in 1228 by the Zen monk Wu-men (1184-1260), it is a collection of 48 koans with Wu-men's own comment in verse and prose.

mushin [no-mind]:   The "true mind" in Buddhism. A totally liberated, enlightened mental state. See *ushin.*

mutō [no-sword]:   In the Yagyū school of swordsmanship, fighting an armed opponent unarmed; in the swordsmanship developed by Yamaoka Tesshū (1836-1888), forgetting the sword and concentrating on the mind.

ō-metsuke [inspector general]: A ranking administrative position during the Tokugawa period (1603-1868) whose principal duty was supervision of the activities of daimyo and the performance of government officials.

sangaku [three learnings]: A Buddhist term referring to the three basic stages of study that must be gone through toward enlightenment.

seishi: See *kishōmon*.

shinmyōken [divine sword]: (1) A fighting technique; (2) that part of the body closest to the hands gripping the hilt of the sword.

shuji shuriken: Separately, *shuji* means a point to mark for attack, and *shuriken*, an accurate assessment of the opponent's stratagem. As a single term, it may mean either *shuji* or *shuriken*.

shuriken: See *shuji shuriken*.

suigetsu [moon on the water]: The distance between two combatants in which each can strike the other; or the act of traversing the distance.

tai [antonym of *yū*]: Noumenon.

tai [antonym of *ken* in the phrase *ken-tai*]: Waiting stance or the state of mind in that stance. Holding back.

tanka: A Japanese poetic form consisting of 31 syllables arranged in the pattern of 5, 7, 5, 7, 7.

tsuke: A move intended to induce the opponent's move.

ushin [be-mind]: The "false mind" in Buddhism. The opposite of *mushin*, which see.

yū: Phenomenon.